PRAISE FOR *SCHOOL OF BOOZE*

'Jane Peyton serves up an intoxicating brew of drinking lore, boozy anecdotes and hop-driven history – this is the sort of school I wish I'd gone to.'

Adrian Tierney-Jones, beer writer and
author of *1001 Beers You Must Taste Before You Die*

'Whether it's the words for "hangover" in Swedish, the beer-related miracles of Brigit of Kildare, or the three classifications of a drunk in Japan, you'll find it all in here, as beer sommelier Jane Peyton takes us on an enjoyable tour of all things alcoholic. Covering all types of drink, from absinthe through to whisky, one swiftly realises that Jane is as much a lover of words and history as she is of booze. Where else will you find the origins of the phrases "fill your boots" and "scot free" within a few pages?

Just like those conversations down the pub, this is a mix of fun, fancy and facts, presented with Jane's refreshing charisma and engaging enthusiasm. You are hereby cordially invited to join the principal of the School of Booze for an entertaining jollification.
Cheers!'

—Susanna Forbes, editor and publisher of DrinkBritain.com

'Jane Peyton's passion for the subject shines through on every page of this riotous, irreverent journey through the world of drink. Chock full of fascinating drinks trivia too.'

—Alice Lascelles, columnist, *The Times of London*,
and founding editor of *Imbibe* magazine

'The perfect starter to a great pub conversation. Will launch a thousand sentences that begin with the words, "I bet you didn't know..."'

Pete Brown, author of *Man Walks into a Pub* and *Hops and Glory*

ALSO BY THE AUTHOR
Beer O'Clock: An Insider's Guide to Craft, Cask and Culture

JANE PEYTON

SCHOOL OF
BOOZE

AN INSIDER'S GUIDE TO
LIBATIONS, TIPPLES *&* BREWS

Skyhorse Publishing

CONTENTS

CHAPTER THREE: RAISE A GLASS TO THE ANCESTORS

CHAPTER FOUR: THE SHOPPING LIST

CHAPTER FIVE: BEHIND THE BAR

CHAPTER SIX: THE OTHER SIDE OF
THE COIN

CHAPTER SEVEN:

PREFACE TO THE NORTH AMERICAN EDITION

Hello North American readers – thank you for buying this book. What are you drinking? Mine's a glass of beer.

Having a 'drink' is an activity that bonds billions of people around the world in friendship. In countries where alcohol is legal most of the places where people appear to be having the most fun are licensed to sell intoxicating liquor. In Britain, where I was born and live, 'going down the pub' is the country's number one leisure activity, and visitors to British shores say that fish and chips and a pint of beer in a traditional British boozer is in the top five things they want to experience during their stay. As well as writing books and running an events company called School of Booze, I also host private tours of historic London pubs. Most clients are American and Canadian and we always have a blast on our pub crawls! As British polymath Dr Samuel Johnson (1709–1784) wrote so appositely, "*There is nothing which has yet been contrived by man, by which so much happiness is produced as by a good tavern or inn.*"

This book was originally commissioned by a publisher in Britain so a number of cultural references and the treatment of some subjects are written from a British point of view.

PREFACE

During my research I was fascinated to learn of the major role that alcohol played in the justification for the American colonies declaring independence from Britain. In British schools we learn of the Boston Tea Party. From what I now know, it should be renamed the Boston Long Island Iced Tea Party. In Canada, hard liquor was currency for fur traders, and during Prohibition much of the decent whisky consumed clandestinely in America came from north of the 49th parallel.

So many significant events in human history are connected with alcohol. If you are a history buff who also likes a snifter or two then this is definitely the book for you!

To your good health.

Jane Peyton
London, UK

INTRODUCTION:
A JOLLIFICATION

Don't tell the social services, but when my siblings and I were children, our parents allowed us to drink a tiny glass of low-alcohol cider with Christmas dinner. It was a once-a-year treat that made the day even more special. We lifted our glass and Dad gave a toast to deceased family members. Then we sipped the sweet sparkling juice knowing that we were participating in a ritual. Even back then I preferred the cider with the pork rather than turkey. A nascent sommelier!

My three wonderful maiden great-aunts used to throw jollifications when the extended family would gather for singing, laughter, and maybe a jig fuelled by something stronger than lemonade. An abiding memory is what fun it all was when people congregated and had a drink. They relaxed, laughed, told jokes, sang, acted daft, and everyone felt the warmth of companionship.

I have always been fascinated by the story behind alcohol – how it is made, the effect it has, the cultural history, and its central role in so many societies. This led me to found an events business called School of Booze. I host tutored beer, cider, wine, whisky tasting events for private groups, appear as a public speaker, and recreate libations from historic eras. My passion is beer and I am an accredited beer sommelier, which if you like beer is one of the most enjoyable things a person can do!

When it comes to the urge for a drink, necessity is the mother of invention. In my experience the greatest example of this is the nomads of Mongolia (and other central Asian countries) who roam around the steppes in search of pasture for their animals. These people would not know what to do with a piece of fruit or a vegetable as they do not stay anywhere long enough to grow anything to eat or supply ingredients to make hooch with. So what do they do when the nearest off-licence may be hundreds of miles away? They drink *airag* (also known as *kumis*) which is made from fermented horse's milk.

Horses play a central role in their society and so does *airag* as an important part of the daily diet. A nineteenth-century book celebrating the nutritional and health qualities of *airag* referred to it as 'milk champagne'. In Mongolia *airag* is also distilled into a clear spirit called *shimiin arkhi*. At around 12 per cent ABV it has a bigger kick than its low alcohol sibling. Fermentation is easy to achieve when airborne yeast cells land on the milk and ferment the sugars, but milking the mare is a little trickier. A foal suckles its mother's teat to start the milk flow and then a milkmaid moves in with a bucket, wraps an arm around the mare's hind leg and starts milking. I can vouch for the fact that *airag* tastes similar to yoghurt with a sour flavour and slight tingle on the tongue because I spent some time in Mongolia. My hosts offered me a drink and, well, it would be rude not to. They passed a bowl, the size of a heavyweight boxer's fist, full of a pale thin liquid. With all eyes on me I accepted it and smiled as I tucked in, trying to avoid the horse hairs floating around on the top, and finished the entire serving. Little did I know that in Mongolia if you eat and drink everything served up, it means you want more.

This book is dedicated to the peerless British boozer and is a guide to what's behind the bar. If you've ever wondered how your favourite drink is made, then this is the book for you.

11

It also includes highlights of the history of some of the most popular alcoholic beverages with compelling pieces of trivia to tell your mates, where else, but down the pub.

It's not the whole story, just an overview because alcohol is such a vast subject it would not all fit into a book that could be lifted without dislocating the back. The content is unapologetically British-centric. When I mention Britain it is sometimes shorthand for England, Wales and Scotland even if it refers to the time before the Act of Union 1707. Sorry, Scots, I do know that Scotland was an independent country before then. I also refer to some historic regions or principalities by their modern geographic locations in Germany or Italy.

The majority of alcohol's history took place before humans developed writing, so historians rely on archaeology if the evidence exists, or assumptions. And the nature of intoxication means that contemporaneous accounts cannot always be trusted. If repeated enough times ale house legends become their own truth and I found many such examples during my research. This will come as no surprise but there is so much rubbish on the Internet! Juicy tales about alcohol are copied from one website to another without any fact checking. This is particularly true of the provenance of a beer style called India Pale Ale. Most sites that mention it contain incorrect information. For the true story, and other beer-related topics, the best source is historian Martyn Cornell, who writes books and a blog called Zythophile and meticulously researches his subject.

Books I really enjoyed reading for research were: *Drink* by Iain Gately (Gotham Books); *Uncorking the Past* by Patrick McGovern (University of California Press); *Intoxication* by Ronald K. Siegel (Park Street Press), and *Beer and Britannia* by Peter Haydon (Sutton Publishing).

INTRODUCTION

Alcoholic drinks all have their own personalities. They also instil certain attitudes or expectations in their tipplers. These are my collective nouns for the imbibers of some popular libations:

Beer: a conviviality
Champagne: a vivaciousness
Wine: a civilisation
Whisky: a kilter
Absinthe: a sorcery
Mezcal: a mariachi
Brandy: a night-cap

My Dad, Bill, was a great raconteur who enjoyed Scotch whisky with a drop of room-temperature water to open it up. '*No need to drown it,*' he would say. In honour of Bill, here is a limerick he taught me:

> *On the chest of a woman from Sale*
> *Was tattooed the price of ale*
> *And on her behind*
> *For the sake of the blind*
> *Was the same information in Braille*

Bottoms up!

PROLOGUE:

A UNIVERSAL LANGUAGE

According to NASA, the Universe is composed of dark energy, dark matter, and atoms which make up bodies such as stars and planets. There is also something unexpected. Deep in interstellar space there is a vast cloud of alcohol composed of ethanol and methanol measuring billions of miles across. It is located at the centre of the Milky Way 26,000 light years or 150 quadrillion miles away from earth. This proximity has raised a fascinating hypothesis about the initial formation of complex carbon molecules on this planet. Did the alcohol build up into carbon polymers and hitch a ride on comet heads that dispersed space dust on to the earth's surface? If so then could it be that the primordial soup in which simple life developed was really a primordial cocktail?

Those single-celled life forms needed energy and this came from sugars. Once ingested, the sugars fermented and created waste products of alcohol and carbon dioxide. Glycolysis, or sugar fermentation, is believed to be the earliest form of energy production used by life on earth so, 3.6 billion years ago, alcohol was a major factor even in a world of primitive bacteria.

Around 100 million years ago the first fruit-bearing trees appeared. For sugar-loving creatures from insects to higher mammals this was the equivalent of an off-licence opening. Sugar oozing from the fruit attracted airborne yeast cells to ferment it so when insects and animals followed their noses to the syrupy prize they gobbled it up and became gently intoxicated on the alcohol that was the by-product of fermentation. Early humans originated in what is now Africa and they lived largely on a diet of fruit. Chemist Steven Benner of the Foundation for Applied Molecular Evolution in Gainesville, Florida, mapped the evolution of DNA sequences that make up the alcohol metabolising enzyme ADH4 and theorised that the ability to metabolise ethanol might have originated in the common ancestor of chimpanzees, gorillas and humans approximately 10 million years ago when higher primates ate fermenting fruit that had fallen off trees giving them an exciting buzz. This was not forbidden fruit, however, and it spurred our ancestors and animals to actively seek it out. Fermentation is highly beneficial because the nutritional value of the food is enhanced with increased amino acid and vitamin levels. Those augmented calories would sustain whoever ate them and help them survive a hostile environment. Fermentation also made the food easier to digest, supplying nutrition and energy that caused the brain to grow larger.

Archaeologists believe that humans started purposely making alcoholic beverages in the Palaeolithic Era between 2.5 million and 20,000 years ago – a more specific timeframe is not possible. Ingredients varied depending on where they lived – palm sap, figs and other fruits in Africa, wild grapes in the Caucasus. Honey was widely available everywhere and so mead would have been an early beverage, if not the first. Later, when it was discovered that root crops and wild cereals could be fermented, almost everything growing in soil was fair game. No one understood what caused food to turn as if by magic into nourishing alcohol so when religion became a part of the human experience, it was understood that alcohol was a gift from the deities and they were worshipped accordingly with libations offered in sacrifice. Even today alcohol is central in some Christian and Jewish rites and wine is mentioned in the holy books as God-given.

So far the earliest evidence found for alcoholic drink is on pottery shards in a Neolithic village in north central China that date back to 7000 BC. When the residue was analysed by biomolecular archaeologist Patrick McGovern he identified fermented rice, honey, wild grapes and hawthorn fruit. Those Chinese tipplers had consumed a rice beer/wine hybrid. The Neolithic was the pottery era when humans started to store food and drink in clay vessels. These left an archaeological record. Before pottery, food and drink were stored in animal stomachs and skins, baskets, or wooden containers all of which rotted away over millennia leaving nothing behind to signal how long humans had been imbibing. Patrick McGovern has a theory that the desire for alcohol changed the habits of hunter-gatherer nomadic humans and made them settle in one place so they could be near the plants used to make their favourite booze. This was the birth of agriculture and of civilisation as people started living in close proximity in settlements, purposely planting crops and working together to harvest them.

Unknown to the drinkers their habits gave them an advantage over the abstemious because fermented food contains beneficial microflora called *Lactobacillus acidophilus* which aid digestion, maintain healthy intestines and boost immune system functions. Alcohol also kills harmful microorganisms in food and water.

Our early drinking ancestors lived longer, and reproduced more. Alcohol's psychotropic effects made them cheerful and less inhibited, encouraged singing, dancing, flirting. Even when the party ended with fighting or face down on the savannah, alcohol's effects were too seductive to resist.

Different cultures throughout the world most likely started drinking independently with no knowledge of the others. But trade and exploration certainly spread the habit and appreciation of this mystic gift of nature. Major routes such as the Silk Road, River Nile, and Great Rift Valley were the equivalent of information superhighways. Alcohol is a social lubricant and helped to build community bonds, ease negotiations, resolve disagreements, seal contracts, commune with deities, perform rituals and celebrate significant events. In many cultures alcohol was, and in many places still is, central to society and features in all communal activities. In English when someone says '*Let's go for a drink*', they do not mean a cup of tea.

Alcohol has been used over millennia as a universal palliative due to medicinal properties such as pain relief, antioxidant, antiseptic, and to fight disease. Ancient societies in Egypt, Mesopotamia, China, Greece and Rome used alcohol internally and externally to treat ailments and also used it as a delivery method in which to dissolve medicinal herbs and spices.

Apart from countries where alcohol is forbidden for religious reasons almost every nation in the world produces some type of booze – most commonly this is pilsener lager (the pale, carbonated style of beer made by brewers such as Heineken and Beck's). Drinking is a custom that knows no cultural or class boundaries – it is a universal language.

In modern society there is no escape from alcohol. It is in countless everyday goods such as perfume, deodorant, mouthwash, and cleaning products. It is even present in the guts of people who consume carbohydrates which is almost everyone on earth. Sugars in food are fermented by intestinal microflora in a process called auto-brewery syndrome. But the amount of alcohol produced is not enough to make a cocktail with, nor is it an excuse to use in court for being over the limit when driving!

CHAPTER ONE:

THE FOURTH DRIVE

IRRESISTIBLE INTOXICATION

Of all human experiences, the English language has more words for the state of inebriation than any other. From ankled to zombied, with expressions such as caned, ganted, glambazzled, lashed, sloshed and trollied coming in between. Try this experiment. Make up a nonsense word then place the suffix '-ed' on the end and say to a friend 'I was completely ****ed last night'. They will understand what you mean and may reply sympathetically 'Oh dear, did you end up photocopying your face on the office copier?'

Could it be true that humans are hard-wired to seek mind-altering substances such as caffeine, tobacco, psychedelic drugs, and alcohol? American psychopharmacologist Dr Ronald Siegel believes so and calls this basic desire for intoxication the 'fourth drive' as fundamental as food, drink and sex. Dr Samuel Johnson, eighteenth-century essayist, recognised it when he described alcohol as life's 'second greatest pleasure'.

Alcohol is the most readily available intoxicant but if it were not then humans would find another source. In his book *The Varieties of Religious Experience* (1902), psychologist William

19

James called alcohol the 'great exciter of yes' and wrote 'The sway of alcohol over mankind is unquestionably due to its power to stimulate the mystical faculties of human nature, usually crushed to earth by the cold facts and dry criticism of the sober hour. Sobriety diminishes, discriminates, and says no; drunkenness expands, unites and says yes. It is in fact the great exciter of the yes function in man.'

So what happens physically when we have a drink? Alcohol enters the bloodstream through the stomach lining and small intestine. If the drink is carbonated or warm (for instance mulled wine) this increases pressure in the stomach and speedily forces alcohol through the pyloric sphincter into the gut where it is absorbed. Food slows the absorption of alcohol which is why when drinking on an empty stomach it has a quicker effect.

Alcohol normally affects women more rapidly than men because they tend to have a higher proportion of body fat. Fat cannot absorb alcohol so it concentrates at higher levels in the blood. Women also have less alcohol dehydrogenase, an enzyme that breaks down alcohol before it enters the bloodstream. Hormonal changes during the menstrual cycle can also affect alcohol metabolism meaning that women become drunker quicker at certain times of the month than others.

Once absorbed the alcohol hits the brain and this is where it becomes so seductive. Ethanol is the soul of alcohol and it affects the central nervous system. In small doses creating euphoria and diminishing inhibitions, in larger quantities slurred speech, drowsiness and impaired motor function. In excessive amounts it can be fatal. The brain's neural pathways are affected, particularly the emotional centres and those concerned with language, music making, and self-consciousness. One minute it is natter, natter, natter, then 'Bohemian Rhapsody' on the karaoke machine, then 'I love you, mate, you're my best friend', followed by tears into the beers, and finally a kebab.

Alcohol triggers the brain chemicals dopamine and serotonin in a reward cascade that makes us feel good, relieves anxiety, and calms frayed nerves. Research conducted by Indiana University School of Medicine revealed surprising results. Even a small sip of a person's favourite drink in such a miniscule quantity that the alcohol would have no effect still generated dopamine. So just the taste, the memory and the anticipation of a drink is enough to prompt happy feelings. Alcohol also releases opioids and these bestow a feeling of elation and provide temporary relief from pain. But alcohol is also a depressive so in excess, and depending on a person's mood and mental state, it may have negative effects.

Alcohol is largely metabolised in the liver with the aid of enzymes called alcohol dehydrogenase (ADH4) and aldehyde dehydrogenase (ALDH). They break it down into acetaldehyde, a toxin that causes hangovers, then to acetate and finally water and carbon dioxide as it is expelled from the body. It takes longer for alcohol to be metabolised than it does to absorb it, so intoxication lasts for some time after a person ceases drinking. Some people have a genetic mutation that prevents the body producing standard levels of ADH4 so they are unable to metabolise acetaldehyde properly and suffer when they drink. This problem is virtually non-existent in the West, but it occurs in up to 40 per cent of people in East Asia causing unpleasant symptoms such as nausea and dizziness. In other words drinkers get an instant hangover. It's enough to put a person off.

Or maybe not. How many times have you said 'never again' the morning after? According to the epigram the definition of insanity is repeating the same action and expecting a different result. So that would suggest people who have ever suffered a hangover are mad if they don't give up drinking. But if the theory of the fourth drive is actuality then humans cannot help themselves in the pursuit of altered states of consciousness.

CARPENTERS IN THE HEAD

In medieval England it was called 'ale passion' (passion then meant 'suffering') and was liable to cause grog blossoms – the little spots that heavy drinkers sometimes suffer from. In France it known as *la gueule de bois* – 'woody mouth'; Germany *Katzenjammer* – 'wailing of the cats'; and in Norway it is *jeg har tommermen* – 'carpenters in the head'. In all those languages it translates as the dreaded hangover with the associated thumping head, nausea, wooziness, shaking, fever, vomiting, and lethargy. Such misery can last for up to two days and only one thing is guaranteed to prevent hangovers – sobriety. Not even the habit in Puerto Rico of rubbing half a lemon or lime under the armpit before a binge will work.

Alcohol is dehydrating; so is all the extra urination that drinking prompts. Dehydration causes headaches and dizziness. Most alcohol also contains toxins called congeners, by-products of fermentation. When alcohol breaks down in the body then acetaldehyde is created, the presence of which initiates a complex chemical reaction that causes all those horrible hangover symptoms. Some people swear hangovers get worse with age – this is probably true and is due to a decline in the levels of the enzyme ADH4 which is responsible for efficient metabolisation of alcohol.

Around one-quarter of drinkers are resistant to hangovers and this is possibly connected with genetic differences in the way the body manages

It is a myth that drinking black coffee will quickly sober a person up. Only time will do that because the body processes alcohol at a specific rate regardless of any interventions such as a shot of espresso. What caffeine most likely does is to make the person more alert and fool them into thinking they are sobering up.

Japanese salarymen are obliged to drink after work with their colleagues even if they do not want to. In such cases to save face they might pretend to be drunk. By doing so they are following a centuries-old tradition in Japan where men are considered ill-mannered if they remain sober at a social event. Drunkenness is tolerated for Japanese men (but not for women) – even the embarrassing behaviour that goes with it. In Japan there are three classifications of drunk – *warai-jogo* (happy drunk); *naki-jogo* (lachrymose drunk); *neji-jogo* (nasty drunk).

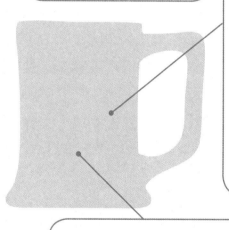

Remember the saying: 'Beer after wine and you'll feel fine; wine after beer and you'll feel queer'? Ignore it because hangovers are caused by the amount imbibed and how the body metabolises alcohol – not the sequence it is consumed in. Darker coloured drinks contain more congeners (toxic compounds) than lighter or clear coloured ones so a bottle or two of red wine after a few pints of stout is enough to make anyone feel queer!

alcohol. For the remainder of drinkers who suffer the effects of over-doing it, they might try restorative food. In Korea people tuck into a bowl of *haejangguk* (translates as 'soup to chase a hangover') a beef broth made with pork, dried cabbage, and ox blood; *menudo* (tripe soup) is a *vuelva a la vida*, or 'come-back-to-life food' in Mexico. Ancient Romans ate fried song birds including canaries, whereas their Greek contemporaries were partial to a dish of sheep lungs and owl eggs. They also thought that boiled cabbage and cabbage seeds would do the trick as did Ancient Egyptians. Little did they know that cabbage contains compounds that reduce the damage of by-products caused as the system copes with the over-indulgence. Pass the sauerkraut.

Researchers at Newcastle University claim that food might really work as a hangover remedy by speeding up the metabolism and helping the body eliminate alcohol more quickly. There may also be some truth in the bacon butty cure that so many Britons turn to. Protein breaks down into amino acids which top up brain chemicals depleted by alcohol thereby making a person feel better.

What has no effect is the hair of the dog – i.e. another drink to repair the damage. It may have a temporary influence but makes things worse by increasing toxins and dehydration serving only to postpone the misery. Take comfort from this incontrovertible truth in the law of hangovers; although today you may feel foul, tomorrow will be gorgeous.

Research studies discovered that people led to believe they have been drinking alcohol exhibit a range of behaviour associated with intoxication including increased aggression, greater confidence, and heightened sexual arousal. It is a condition called false intoxication.

In the fifth-century BC Persian statecraft relied on alcohol. Important decisions were taken through group debate oiled by plenty of wine. If when sober the following day discussion resulted in the same conclusion, the policy was adopted. Conversely, choices made when sober were also debated when drunk to see what the verdict was.

It is often said that drinking alcohol through a straw makes a person get drunk faster. The reality is that it has no effect on the speed of intoxication. Perhaps the myth arose because the alcoholic beverages people normally drink through a straw are fruity or sweet so they go down quicker. And when drinking through a straw it is harder to tell how much liquid is in the mouth – usually a gulp rather than a sip.

MONKEYING AROUND – ANIMALS AND ALCOHOL

Humans are just one species of animal enamoured of alcohol. Most land-based creatures in the wild from insects to elephants seek out over-ripe fruit for a tasty sugary cocktail loaded with energy and nutrients. In small animals, intoxication is a side effect but does not deter them. They may even remember the peculiar feeling and go back for more. And like humans who know about the dangers of over-doing it, some animals instinctively know when to cut down. Take female lab hamsters with access to alcohol. Normally they prefer a drink of 10 per cent ABV rather than water. But when pregnant or nursing they significantly reduce their alcohol intake, only increasing it again once their offspring are weaned.

Other laboratory animals fed with alcohol display behaviour that is similar to human traits of drinking. In one lab, chimps that had unlimited alcohol consumed the equivalent of three or four bottles of wine in a session with males drinking more than females. Over time, as they got used to it, they did not binge but still drank enough to be permanently drunk. They preferred sweet wines over dry.

A primate known as the Malaysian tree shrew has nightly binges on fermented palm nectar with an alcohol content of around 3.8 per cent. This is a symbiotic relationship because as the shrews gorge on the flowers they pollinate the plant. Throughout the night they can consume the equivalent of nine glasses of wine yet are such hardened drinkers they show no signs of intoxication as they go from tree to tree.

Insects' natural attraction to alcohol is well known. Fruit flies know to lay their eggs where there are intense odours of alcohol as when fruit is fermenting this guarantees larvae a source of sugar and high-protein yeast for food. Butterfly and moth collectors spread beer, sugar and rum on tree trunks and it attracts swarms that can then be trapped. For slugs caught in a beer trap it is a one-way journey as they end up drowning having been enticed by the aroma. Compare this to the rats in parts of Africa that are tempted by bowls of milk mixed with beer left out at night by villagers. It is simple to pick up the inebriated rats the next day and dispose of them.

With birds in the wild it is not uncommon for them to die en masse after feasting on fermenting berries. Scientists have examined avian corpses and found high levels of ethanol in the liver meaning that the cause of death was alcohol poisoning.

In similar conditions with an all-they-can-drink buffet, rats showed greater self-control than chimps did and quickly adopted rituals. Just before feeding time the rats gathered around a drinking hole for a pre-dinner snifter. Then a couple of hours later had one for the road before going to sleep. Every few days they would binge as though it were the weekend. Some heavy-drinking rats displayed symptoms of alcoholism drinking early in the morning, eating less, staying in their burrows and being anti-social. Then when alcohol was removed from the colony they showed signs of withdrawal. After a few weeks of not drinking, the alcoholics reverted to normal rat behaviour.

In Africa fermenting fruit from palm trees acts like a beacon as it sends out odour across the savannah that animals pick up on the wind. Elephants do not normally expend unnecessary calories but palm fruit is an irresistible delicacy for which it is worth walking miles. Once they have found it they shake the trees until the fruit falls. In the gut, the fruit continues to ferment and the elephant's behaviour may change as they are easily startled, and become excitable and aggressive. Ancient societies used elephants in war and they were fed with alcohol to calm them down or to inspire courage in battle. Roman writer Pliny noted: '*When captured they are quickly tamed by the juice of barley*'.

A tantalising treat in Malaysia and Sumatra is the durian fruit. It contains sweet custard that ferments and attracts orang-utan, monkeys, bears, and squirrels to pick it from the tree. As the fruit ripens and falls to the ground it splits open to reveal alcoholic pulp which rhino, elephants, deer, pigs, tapirs, ants, beetles, and humans vie for. Flying foxes also gorge on it but the alcohol affects their sonar and they fall out of the air and end up stumbling on the ground until they sober up. But of all creatures seeking fermented fruit, the durian-fanatic tigers are the most dangerous. They have been known to attack humans carrying baskets of the fruit and nick it, sometimes killing as they do so.

DOWN THE HATCH – TOASTING

Drinking has always been imbued with ritual. Even now when we raise a glass to a friend or member of the group it is done with reverence, as an acknowledgment of a shared experience, to create good feeling and as a means of bonding.

Throughout history various cultures have used alcohol intoxication as a way of communing with their deities. By offering up their drink as a sacrifice they displayed their devotion.

In ancient Greece worshippers performed a libation – this was the name of the ritual where a glass of wine was shared with the gods. They stood up and looked to the skies, recited a prayer and raised the glass, deliberately spilling a little wine as an offering before drinking it. Today as a formal toast, the group stands up and raises a glass as they repeat the name of the toastee. Not too different from a libation from antiquity.

Toasting someone for good health was common in ancient Rome where a piece of toast was dropped into wine.

Charcoal in the burned bread was believed to reduce the acidity of wine making it more palatable. The Latin term *tostus* translates as roasted or scorched – hence the word toast. A toast was considered so important that the Senate decreed all citizens must drink to the health of the emperor before each meal.

For many Christians one of the most important rituals in worship is the Eucharist, or Holy Communion, where bread and wine are offered up to God in remembrance of the Last Supper when Jesus Christ gave thanks, held up the wine towards heaven, and then shared it with his friends.

In societies where enemies might be offed with poison, a symbol of friendship was for the host to pour the drinks from a communal pitcher, take the first mouthful and then raise his glass for guests to do likewise. This was a guarantee that the drinks were not spiked. So next time someone buys you a drink make sure you say 'I'll have what she's having'.

From the late seventeenth century onwards if someone in England or Scotland raised a toast to the 'King Over the Water' it meant they supported the Stuart king, James II, and his heirs. In 1688 he had been replaced on the throne by his daughter Mary and her husband William of Orange. James went into exile, over the water in France. Jacobites would gather in taverns and alehouses to drink and sing subversive songs about restoring the Stuarts. At formal occasions during the loyal toast when the monarch was toasted, Jacobites would silently pass their glass over a beaker of water.

England's restoration of the monarchy in 1660 was celebrated so heartily that the king, Charles II, was forced to issue 'A Proclamation Against Vicious, Debauch'd and Profane Persons' saying 'There are likewise a set of men of whom we have heard much, who spend their time in taverns and tippling houses and debauches, giving no other evidence of affection for us but in drinking our health, and in inveigling against all others who are not of their own dissolute temper.' Toasting was a patriotic duty and a release after the strictures of the Puritan era. Romantics would pledge fidelity to their beloved by toasting her with the same number of glasses of wine as there were letters in her name. Or for a more dramatic flourish stab themselves in the arm and mix blood with wine and drink to the object of their desire. Individuals who earned multiple toasts became known as the 'Toast of the Town'.

CHAPTER TWO:

BOOZE: PART OF THE FURNITURE

WHAT THE DOCTOR ORDERED – ALCOHOL AND HEALTH

> *'Wine is a food, a medicine, and a poison;*
> *it's just a question of dose.'*
> Paracelsus, sixteenth-century Swiss
> physician and alchemist

This is the paradox – alcohol in moderation can be beneficial to health and society, be a source of pleasure and contentment, but too much and it can cause chronic disease, alcoholism, social problems and even death.

Throughout history, alcohol has been used knowingly and sometimes unwittingly as medicine, delivering health benefits with its antiseptic and analgesic properties. Upper Nile Nubians in the early years of the first millennium were not to know that the grain they used for brewing beer was impregnated with the bacteria *Streptomyces*, which is used today to make antibiotic medication. American anthropologists who studied bones of people from that area discovered evidence of the bacteria and concluded it had protected them from certain diseases.

Further down the Nile in Egypt beer was used internally and externally to treat a range of ailments ranging from gum disease, as a dressing for wounds (if the grain there also contained *Streptomyces* then a beer poultice would have been just the thing), and even as an anal fumigant when beer vapour was used to treat piles, worms and other problems of the rear end. An unknown Egyptian physician wrote that '*Hekt* (beer) is the liquid of happy blood and body'.

Ancient Greeks were devoted to drinking wine, not just as a mark of civilisation but as a useful item in the pharmacopoeia. Depending on the medical problem, specific wines would be used to treat cancer, sweeten the breath, calm wind, and prevent constipation. But beware wine from the region of Heraia which had the reputation of making 'women inclined to pregnancy'.

Roman naturalist Pliny the Elder (AD 23–79) wrote that beer froth 'nourishes the skin in the faces of women'. Remember the TV advert for 'Boddington's – Cream of Manchester' where a beautiful model carefully massages beer onto her face and her boyfriend says 'By 'eck, you smell gorgeous, petal'? Pliny was right! Another Roman writer, Cato extensively documented medicinal uses for wine especially when mixed with herbs. He was partial to juniper (the main botanical in gin) infused in wine which was prescribed for gout and as a topical treatment for snakebites. Tapeworms would be made history by drinking wine mixed with pomegranate juice. A foolproof laxative was believed to be a cocktail of wine, manure, ashes and herbs. Wine was a panacea with magical ability to cure virtually all physical and mental health problems and in parts of the Italian peninsula this belief lasted well into the Renaissance.

One of the first applications of distillation was to create medicines from fruits, herbs and flowers. Distilled grapes and cereal became known as *eau de vie* or *aqua vitae* – water of life – and for centuries it was consumed for medicinal benefits. It just happened to hit the spot as well. Monasteries in medieval Europe became mini medical labs as monks and nuns experimented with elixirs. One alcoholic herbal remedy invented by holy orders, Chartreuse, is still produced today.

It has long been recognised that the French, who eat a lot of saturated fat in cream, butter, and meat, are less likely to suffer heart disease than other nationalities in the West. Termed the 'French Paradox', regular consumption of red wine is believed to account for it because grapes contain antioxidants and polyphenols, and the alcohol which promotes 'good' cholesterol increases coronary blood flow and reduces blood pressure.

Other alcoholic drinks can be beneficial in moderation – particularly beer. Around the world in dozens of independent studies by respected medical foundations the results suggest that moderate drinking is associated with healthier and longer lives when compared to abstainers or alcohol abusers.

Just as with red wine, research shows that drinking beer can reduce the risk of

> Alcohol is often described as having 'empty calories', i.e. no nutritional value. Technically that is true but it is misleading because people do not consume pure alcohol, they drink alcoholic beverages. These are not only nutritious due to the ingredients they are made from – grapes, apples, cereals for example – but during fermentation that nutrition increases in value. Beer for instance contains protein, amino-acids, vitamins (lots in the B complex), minerals – in particular silicon, magnesium, iron, and potassium. It is also an excellent source of soluble fibre. So forget muesli – drink beer for breakfast!

No matter the language, a fat stomach is universally known as a 'beer belly'. But medical studies have revealed that people who do not drink beer are just as likely to get a belly as those who *do* drink beer. Kebab belly, fish and chips belly, or lack of exercise belly is more accurate. Blame a person's lifestyle because weight gain is caused by more calories going in than being worked off as physical activity. In calories, beer is lower than the equivalent of fruit juice or wine. A pint of beer of around 4 per cent ABV contains approximately 190 calories, a pint of orange juice 256 calories, and a pint of white wine contains approximately 405 calories. Beer contains no fat or cholesterol but unfortunately it demands that fatty snacks are consumed as an accompaniment. A 100 gram packet of peanuts contains 600 calories, then there are the pork scratchings, crisps, pie and chips, burgers, curry, and the mandatory kebab on the way home from the pub.

heart disease and stroke. Hops contain antioxidants that can prevent bad cholesterol from damaging arteries. Those helpful little flowers also contribute to a lowered risk of gallstones, kidney stones, bone fractures, osteoporosis, and type II diabetes.

Unfortunately the media is dominated by reports of binge drinking and the problems it causes to health and society, so reports on the benefits of a sensible intake of alcohol are not as widely broadcast. A surprising champion is the United States Center for Disease Control that declares moderate consumption of alcohol, non-smoking, a nutritious diet, and regular exercise are 'four healthy lifestyle behaviors that exert a powerful and beneficial effect on mortality'. So to quote the Russian proverb: 'Drink a glass of schnapps after your soup and you steal a rouble from the doctor'. Or as the French would say over a glass of wine – *à votre santé*.

GOD-GIVEN – RELIGION AND ALCOHOL

Wine is central to the rituals of Judaism and Christianity and mentioned in the holy books of those religions as a divine gift – a source of happiness. In the Old Testament of the Bible, wine is a God-given libation but it warns that drunkenness leads to bad behaviour and over-indulgence is shameful. The New Testament celebrates that Jesus Christ was a wine drinker. It is a joy-bringing symbol to be consumed in moderation and never abused. Wine even had a starring role in Jesus's first miracle when he turned water into wine at the wedding of Cana.

Some Jews sanctify the Sabbath by reciting a blessing over wine, and before bed use a few drops to extinguish a ceremonial candle. During the Passover meal four glasses of wine must be consumed, each with symbolic meaning. In the Christian Eucharist wine is offered in remembrance of the Last Supper and to symbolise the blood of Jesus. But for some branches of the Christian faith alcohol is so repugnant that wine is not even used in worship, never mind actually consumed, and grape juice is used instead.

According to the Old Testament, Noah was the first vintner who after the great flood planted vines on Mount Ararat. Then he tasted the wine and this is what happened: *'He drank of the wine, and was drunken; and he was uncovered in his tent'* (Genesis 9:21).

If those teetotallers had lived in the early days of Christianity they would have been branded heretics because wine was fundamental to doctrine so abstinence was akin to heresy. There was a sect of Christians who chose not to drink and church leaders eventually accepted their decision as long as the symbolism of wine remained in the holy rituals. Ascetic missionaries spreading Christianity in Europe in the Dark Ages gradually realised that to convert the pagans their drinking habits must be tolerated and if you can't beat 'em, join 'em.

Several saints and holy people are credited with beer-related miracles but the most prolific was an Irish woman, St Brigid of Kildare (c.450–523), who turned water into beer on several occasions including changing the bathwater at a leper colony into good red ale. Another time she prayed over the brew and it multiplied to provide enough ale to last through Holy Week.

In the pantheon of Catholic saints, drinkers should revere the multi-tasking St Armand, patron saint of beer, brewers, publicans, bartenders, hopgrowers, winemakers, and vintners. And boy scouts for good measure.

Existing pagan festivals were assimilated and rebranded into Christian feast days such as Christmas and these were an excuse for a shindig. All was going swimmingly until the medieval period when with the rise of alehouses, people stayed in the pub instead of going to mass. Something had to be done and so the Church decided to classify inebriation as gluttony which meant it was one of the seven deadly sins. This may have prompted more people to go to mass but it did not stop them from getting sozzled on occasion because after all, according to the Bible, alcohol was a gift from God.

As long as the faithful drank moderately it was not a problem. Good job too because in northern Europe religious orders came to brewing as though they were born to it. Christian duty meant that abbeys and monasteries must provide sustenance – beer, bread, and a bed to pilgrims travelling to holy sites. This is the origin of the inn. Monks and nuns were allowed to drink beer even on fasting days when only bread and water was permitted – after all it is liquid bread – their ration was eight pints of strong beer a day. Today several breweries have direct connections with their religious past, the Trappist beers and Leffe in Belgium, and Germany's Weihenstephan, the world's oldest beer brand still brewed on its original site (founded in AD 1040).

And it was not just beer – monasteries became proficient at distilling, making mead, and in places where vines grew, monks and nuns practised viticulture. Cistercian monks in particular were adept and they founded monasteries all over Europe spreading their expert wine knowledge wherever they settled. Benedictine monks at Buckfast Abbey, Devon, made an eponymous fortified tonic wine in the 1890s advertised with the slogan 'Three small glasses a day, for good health and lively blood'. It is no longer made by monks but is produced under licence elsewhere and now laced with caffeine and sugar. Its subtle bouquet is highly esteemed by Glaswegian teenagers in bus shelters where it is known as Buckie, Commotion Lotion, and Wreck the Hoose Juice.

DOWN THE PUB

Shebeen, bar, café, brasserie, bodega, lodge, inn, saloon, tavern, or beer hall – better known in Britain as the pub. A pub is so much more than just a place to go for a drink, it is a community resource, a place for socialising, gossiping, building bonds, flirting, commiserating, and celebrating in. They form a fragment of the DNA of British life so when a pub closes it is death by a thousand cuts to the social health of the nation.

When the Romans landed in Albion in AD 43 they found the natives happily supping ale, mead, and cider but just round at their mates' rather than in a building dedicated to drinking. The Roman occupiers constructed an extensive network of roads to move troops around the country. Rest stops called *tabernae* which sold wine and food were built along the highways. *Taberna* keepers hung a vine or a bush outside to attract attention and indicate they were open for business. Publicans still do that today with signs and in the medieval era anyone selling beer had to hang an ale-stake from their premises as a signal that ale was sold there. It was not for the convenience of the customer but rather for the ale-conner who had to taste the ale to ensure quality.

The ale-stake was a pole to which a garland of vegetation was attached. Modern pubs with bush in their names probably derived from the tradition of the ale-stake which in turn started with the Romans and the vine. It is plausible that some of the inns along modern

Staleybridge near Manchester holds a record as being home to pubs with the shortest and longest names in Britain. The Q Inn, and The Old Thirteenth Cheshire Astley Volunteer Rifleman Corps Inn.

routes that follow ancient roads have been on that site since Roman times. Thank you, Rome, for introducing one of the most prized institutions any culture could wish for – the pub. As lexicographer, essayist, and member of the booze brigade Dr Samuel Johnson wrote in the eighteenth century, 'No sir, there is nothing which has yet been contrived by man, by which so much happiness is produced as by a good tavern or inn'.

England has never been shy of purloining other cultures' traditions – even language – the English lexicon incorporates words of around 145 other tongues from Afrikaans and 'trek' to Zulu with 'impala'. When the Saxons started settling the country in the fifth century AD they brought their custom of drinking in special halls that were the centre of social and business life. Vikings also drank in halls and they reinforced this convention when they invaded Britain in later centuries.

In the medieval era when drinking ale was often a matter of life or death in areas where the water could not to be trusted, ale was made in domestic dwellings by women – alewives or brewsters. Any surplus might be sold to passers-by – often by a middleman (female) called a huckster. It was common for customers to enter the alewife's home and sit on a bench to drink her ale. This 'public' house eventually became known as a 'pub'. Publicans still live above the shop and continue that tradition of inviting the public into their house.

The Black Death peaked in Britain in 1348–1350 and had the unexpected effect of increasing the consumption of ale. Mortality was so high during the plague that the labour pool shrank and there were fewer healthy people available for work. Those of working age were in such demand they could name their price and so wages improved. Suddenly they had disposable income to spend on ale. Brewsters could not accommodate the thirsty hordes and purposely built alehouses began to flourish. Not

everyone was happy about this – especially the king. Men were spending so much time boozing that they failed to practise long bow at the butts as they were duty bound to do. England had no standing army at the time and there was an enemy across the Channel that regularly required a seeing to. Edward III banned pub games such as dice and cards and men were forced back out on Sunday afternoons to hone their archery skills. Alehouses were not beloved by the ruling classes because they feared the common man would plot and discuss grievances leading to insurrection.

Pictorial pub signs were essential in a time when most people were illiterate. Pubs were generally named after animals, monarchs, saints, tools or other motifs that could easily be represented in a drawing. The most common pub name in Britain varies depending on who is counting, but the Red Lion, Crown, White Hart and Royal Oak are contenders.

They had a point – it is doubtful the Peasants' Revolt of 1381 was planned in a church pew.

Alehouses were blamed by the elite as the root of all evil where an atmosphere of moral turpitude encouraged work-shy wastrels, and were a sanctuary for petty criminals. Sound familiar? They were even blamed for helping to spread syphilis. Throughout the centuries successive kings, queens, and Lord Protector Oliver Cromwell attempted to improve society by supressing alehouses or banning singing, dancing, gambling and cock-fighting within them. Nothing they tried worked – alehouses were far too much fun to lose. Besides they served more than one function – some were used as coroners' courts, prisons, mortuaries, pawnbrokers, and employment bureaux where men with specific trades would let it be known they were available for work – hence pub names such as The Carpenters' Arms.

It was a different story for taverns and inns. They were not considered to be dens of iniquity although neither were they places of virtue. Taverns originally sold only food and wine, not ale, and were patronised by a wealthy clientele of nobles, merchants, lawyers. Customers may have been more affluent but it did not make their behaviour any better than hoi polloi in the alehouses. If reports of the habit of employing small boys to sit under tables and loosen the cravats of comatose men who slumped to the tavern floor are not true then they should be!

Inns had evolved from Roman *tabernae*, largely patronised by travellers especially those visiting holy sites. Hospitality was a

Christian duty and monasteries and abbeys were overwhelmed by pilgrims so institutions were built offering drink, food, beds, and stabling for horses and carriages. Hostler or ostler is another word for a groom or stable boy – this is where the term 'hostelry' in connection with an inn derives.

Thomas Beckett's shrine in Canterbury was a popular destination for pilgrimage and literature's best known pilgrims in Chaucer's *Canterbury Tales* began their journey at The Tabard, an inn that really existed in London's Southwark district. As roads improved so more people started travelling and stage coaches connected major towns and cities. Service stations (known as coaching inns), where not only food, drink and accommodation were offered, also supplied a facility where weary horses could be swapped for fresh ones. Historically the average distance between inns was seven miles so horses were not worn out pulling the heavy loads. Coaching inns were often interchanges where travellers could alight from one coach and wait for another service. News, gossip, and innovations were disseminated this way as people passed through. With the coming of rail, coaching inns declined but this latest mode of transport led to a new breed of public house at railway stations. Several Tube stations on the London Underground are named after pubs including the Angel, Swiss Cottage, Royal Oak, and Manor House.

Circle bars were devised by engineer Isambard Kingdom Brunel – the first was at the buffet in Swindon railway station – as the most efficient method of serving large numbers of people. Until that point most drinking establishments did not have a bar, just a servery hatch through which jugs of ale and cider were passed.

Gin had caused such social problems in cities that the government tried a new ploy and passed the Beerhouse Act 1830. This cancelled duty on beer and authorised any householder who paid for a licence to open a pub and brew or sell beer. Opening hours were permitted between 5 a.m. and 10 p.m. The result was that thousands of pubs starting trading and rather than the population being inebriated on gin, it was beer. With so much competition for customers, pubs had to be creative. Those that could afford to (usually brewing companies) built or refurbished premises in spectacular style with opulent interiors, etched mirrors, high-quality wood carving, mosaics, tiles, gas lighting. Separate booths led off the central circular bar and these catered for women, and people who did not want to fraternise with the lower classes. Nicknamed 'gin palaces', they transported their clientele, usually

In early 1915 when future British Prime Minister David Lloyd George was Chancellor, he told the Shipbuilding Employers Federation that Britain was 'fighting Germans, Austrians and drink, and so far as I can see, the greatest of these three deadly foes is drink' and 'drink is doing more damage than all the German submarines put together'. As a long-term teetotaller he was horrified that pubs were open for nineteen hours a day and most beer was around 7 per cent ABV (much stronger than it is today). A Newcastle shipyard owner had told Lloyd George that men's wages had gone up so much that their double overtime for Sunday working meant they often didn't come in on a Monday. When the Defence of the Realm (Amendment) (No. 3) Act was passed in May 1915 it had a huge impact by restricting pub opening hours to five and a half hours a day – noon to 2.30 p.m. and 6 p.m. to 9 p.m. Although intended to be temporary, limited pub hours continued until 2005. The alcohol level of beer was reduced because enemy submarines patrolling the Atlantic affected imports of grain and home grown cereals were needed for food. British brewers had less malt to use in the beer and that meant lower strength – 3 per cent ABV was the usual.

Other policies led to duty on alcohol being dramatically increased, which hit people in the pocket. The government even outlawed the long-standing habit in British pubs of buying rounds. It became an offence with punishment of a fine or up to six months' imprisonment for anyone caught purchasing a drink for anyone other than themselves. Bar staff were also at risk of being fined for knowingly selling the extra drink as was the person who accepted it. The intention was to reduce consumption of alcohol. In a few areas of the country with massive armament operations (such as Carlisle and Gretna on the Scottish border, and at Enfield in Middlesex), the government nationalised local pubs and breweries in a programme called the State Management Scheme. This was done to control the drinking habits of workers whose labour was essential to make munitions.

the urban poor, into a fantasy world. For the price of a drink, customers entered dreamland. This pub format was known as vertical drinking – no seats, no food, no dawdling. By the Edwardian era when suburbs radiated from towns and cities, a romantic version of Olde England was fashionable in pub building – a medieval pastiche known as 'Brewer's Tudor'. Take a look on main roads in the outskirts of towns – half-timbered pubs proliferate.

The First World War was a distinct boundary from what had gone before as society changed in the post-war era. Life could never be the same – not least because so many young men had perished. Urban slums were razed, council houses built, living conditions improved, and there was more choice of leisure activities. Whilst this was not nirvana it meant that poorer people did not find solace in Gin Lane to escape their miserable lives the way their forebears had in the eighteenth and nineteenth centuries. Thousands of the more squalid boozers closed and were either demolished or changed purpose. But men still wanted to escape to the pub and drink in a male-dominated environment. However, the government and some brewing companies had their own ideas and wanted to turn pubs into family-friendly venues with food, soft drinks, and recreation such as playgrounds. Many hostelries were modernised in a programme known as 'Improved Pubs'. New pubs built on housing estates followed this model too but usually had no atmosphere and were/are generally unloved.

Pub building was halted during the Second World War. In the post-war era of rationing and austerity followed by the modernist 1960s, new builds were little more than functional boxes. Gin palaces were either razed or refurbished and the fantasy vision and craftsmanship of Victorian pubs ended up in skips. The 1980s

Before Britain had a professional army and navy of volunteers, fit men of fighting age were 'joined up' against their will by groups of ruffians called press gangs who received a bounty for each man they delivered. This was especially rife in the eighteenth and early nineteenth centuries when Britain was so often at war. For men to go out drinking in port towns was a risk because press gangs operated with impunity looking for suitable targets and woe betide any young drunk who accepted a drink from a stranger. A shilling may be slipped into their pocket or tankard. By unwittingly accepting the coin, they were hauled away because they had 'taken the King's shilling' and agreed to join the army or navy.

It is a myth, however, that glass-bottomed tankards were designed so men could see if anyone had dropped a coin into their drink and avoid being pressed.

British drinkers owe thanks to Magna Carta (Latin for Great Charter) issued in 1215 – the cornerstone of liberty in the English-speaking world. It laid down certain legal principles and controlled the power of the monarch. Proof of how important ale and wine were in medieval England is in clause 35 which noted 'There shall be standard measures of wine, ale, and corn throughout the kingdom'. People selling short measures might end up in the stocks or, if they were women, be ducked in the village pond.

Leather tankards were commonly used as drinking vessels because they were inexpensive, practical and long lasting. In England they were known as 'jacks' or 'boots'. Which is where the toast 'fill your boots' originates.

was the decade of theme pubs when ersatz Irish boozers landed on high streets of cities and towns across the country. Apart from Guinness on the bar the most authentic Irish connection was the shamrock decoration.

Girl power arrived in the 1990s when pubs were designed with a female customer in mind, changing them from dark dodgy drinking dens with disgusting loos to attractive settings that women would want to spend time and money in. Gone were opaque windows – transparent glass was installed because most women are reluctant to walk in somewhere unless they can first see in from the outside. Beer-sodden carpets were replaced with clean stripped wooden floors, sofas and armchairs installed, and lighting improved. This was also the decade of the gastro pub when menus of food that would not be out of place in a Michelin-starred restaurant replaced microwaved chicken in a basket.

Some people rue the loss of the traditional 'wet' boozer, i.e. no frills, and no food apart from pork scratchings. But pubs like that rarely survive in an era of high beer taxes, no smoking, and changes in drinking habits and leisure time. The bad news is that many pubs are closing – a particular tragedy when the only pub in the village ceases trading. The good news is that the ones that survive have high-quality beer, wine, spirits, food and service. But this is a case of use it or lose it otherwise the warning written in the early twentieth century by Anglo-French writer Hilaire Belloc will come true:

From the towns all inns have been driven: from the villages most...
Change your hearts or you will lose your inns and you will deserve to
have lost them. But when you have lost your inns drown your empty
selves, for you will have lost the last of England.

So get thee to the pub – it's the patriotic duty of everyone in Britain! Some pub names aren't what they appear at first sight and often have a secret meaning or a story behind their moniker.

Bear and Ragged Staff:

This is the heraldic sign of the Earl of Warwick. According to legend the second Earl killed a bear with a ragged staff (a knobbly stick). Pubs most likely took this name in honour of Richard Neville – the powerful fifteenth-century Earl.

Boot and Flogger:

A boot is a leather tankard or bottle and a flogger is a device for hammering a cork into a bottle.

Black Horse:

Legend grew around eighteenth-century highwayman Dick Turpin and his horse Black Bess. Hence the proliferation of pubs named after that trusty steed.

Bull and Bush:

In 1544 King Henry VIII was victorious in a battle at the major French port of Boulogne. The harbour was known as Boulogne Bouche – try saying it in an *'Allo 'Allo* French accent.

Cat and Fiddle:

There are several theories about the origin of this name – (1) it refers to a man called Caton who was a loyal fourteenth-century governor of Calais when the French town was an English possession. His nickname was *Caton le Fidèle*; (2) it was named for a faithful cat *le Chat Fidèle*; or (3) it was in honour of the devout wife of Henry VIII, Catherine of Aragon a.k.a. *Catherine la Fidèle*.

Chequers (or Checkers):

Heraldic signs often feature a chequered pattern so this pub name could refer to the coat of arms of a local landowner. In ancient Rome a chequer board sign was an indication that a tavern also provided banking services. A chequered board was used for counting money on. That is why the premier money maven in the British government is known as Chancellor of the Exchequer.

Cock:

Although the sign usually features a male hen the name refers either to the stopcock (tap) on a beer barrel, or cockfighting as this was a popular pub sport.

Cross Keys:

Keys are the symbol of St Peter, the gatekeeper of heaven.

I am the Only Running Footman:

This is the title of a novel by American writer Martha Grimes and is also a pub in London's Mayfair. When a horse-drawn coach was the fastest mode of transport a footman would run ahead and pay tolls, or carry a torch in darkness.

Lamb and Flag:

This is a religious symbol in which the lamb is the *Agnus Dei* and the cross represents the Christian symbol of Jesus Christ's death. A lamb holding a flag also appears on the coat of arms of the Worshipful Company of Merchant Taylors.

Marquis of Granby:

John Manners, Marquis of Granby, a military commander during the Seven Years' War (1756–1763) provided pensions for his soldiers after they returned to civilian life and many of them bought pubs and named them after their benefactor. The original pub of this name is in the Lincolnshire village of Granby; it is owned by the nearby Brewsters' Brewing Company and sells a range of their ace beers.

Moon under Water:

George Orwell wrote an essay about his perfect pub and named it the Moon under Water.

Percy Arms:

Percy is the family name of the Duke of Northumberland and he owns land in a number of areas of Britain.

Pig and Whistle:

A piggin, or pigkin is a drinking vessel made of leather and the word may be a corruption of pig skin. Two theories vie to explain the origin of 'whistle'. One is that workers in heavy industry would whistle for the water boy to come and bring them a piggin of water. The other is that whistle comes from *wæs hæl*, an Old English expression for 'good health'.

Red Lion:

A red lion is a common heraldic motif so the origin of the name could vary depending on where the pub is. Perhaps it originally related to the coat of arms of a local landowner; in other parts of the country it might have been connected with the personal crest of John of Gaunt, the immensely powerful son of fourteenth-century King Edward III. When James VI of Scotland became James I of England in 1603 he brought the heraldic red lion of Scotland with him and its image started appearing on public buildings.

Rose and Crown:

This relates to the Tudor rose, symbol of the British monarchy.

Royal Oak:

During the English Civil War (1651) the future King Charles II evaded capture after defeat at the battle of Worcester by hiding in an oak tree in a wood in Shropshire. His enemies searched in vain giving Charles the opportunity to escape to France where he lived in exile. The tree became known as the Boscobel Oak (after a nearby house in which Charles sheltered). The 29 May 1660 was declared a public holiday to celebrate the Restoration of the Monarchy and as this was also Charles' birthday it has been known since as Royal Oak or Oak Apple Day.

Saracen's Head and Turk's Head:

During the Crusades, Saracens and Turks were the enemy of the Christians heading to Jerusalem to save the Holy Land from the infidel.

Strangers' Bar:

Alas this is not a public house, it is one of the bars in the Houses of Parliament open only to MPs, parliamentary staff and their guests. The good thing is that if an MP invites a stranger in, they are not permitted to go to the bar so the MP has to buy the drinks.

Swan With Two Necks:

Swans on open waters in Britain are the property of the Crown but in the sixteenth century Queen Elizabeth granted rights to some swans on the River Thames to two London livery companies – the Worshipful Company of Dyers and the Worshipful Company of Vintners. To identify which swans belonged to whom, their beaks were marked or nicked. Two nicks meant they were the vintners' swans.

Three Kings:

The three wise men (Magi) who brought gifts to Jesus in Bethlehem.

White Hart:

In 1393 King Richard II passed a law that made pub signs compulsory so the official ale-conner knew which premises were selling ale and could go and taste it for quality. If the publican failed to hang a sign the penalty was forfeiture of their ale. Richard's heraldic symbol was a white hart (stag) and hundreds of pubs adopted it.

White Horse:

When George, Elector of Hanover became King George I of Britain the white horse became a popular pub name as landlords displayed the equine symbol of the House of Hanover as a sign of loyalty to the new monarch. A rampant white horse is also the symbol of the county of Kent.

In the medieval era skilled craftsmen joined trade guilds or livery companies that had great power and influence. All guilds had coats of arms and many pubs with the word 'three' in their name were inspired by the heraldic symbols or the activities of a local guild. Here are a few such popular pub names:

Three Arrows:

Inspired by either the Worshipful Company of Bowyers (longbow makers) or the Fletchers (arrow makers).

Three Bucks:

From the arms of the Worshipful Company of Leathersellers.

Three Compasses:

Related to the Worshipful Company of Carpenters (geometrical compasses rather than navigational compass).

Three Horseshoes:

From the arms of the Worshipful Company of Farriers.

Three Tuns:

From the Worshipful Company of Brewers, or the Worshipful Company of Vintners.

Three Wheatsheafs:

Inspired by the Worshipful Company of Bakers.

THE VERBALS

A number of common English phrases originate in beer or brewing.

Bridal – everything connected with nuptials. The word originated from 'bride ale'. Ale was an old English term for a celebration – as well as being the word for beer. The bride ale was the marriage feast for which a special beer was brewed. Guests paid to drink this brew and the money went to the newlyweds to help them start off their married life together.

Grist for the mill – meaning something of advantage. In beer terms, grist is the malt that is ground in a mill to be made ready for the mash. Definitely an advantage to the brewer!

Scot free – means escaping punishment. Scot is an old Norse word that meant tax or payment. It probably came into the English lexicon from the Vikings. Its relationship to beer is that in thirteenth-century England the clergy would organise compulsory events called 'church ales' where parishioners had to buy specially brewed beer to raise funds for the Church. Church ales were not as much fun as the ad hoc parties that parishioners organised in the forest outside the jurisdiction of the Church. The authorities could but glower as the people got off 'scot free' and donated nothing to parish coffers. In revenge the government was persuaded by the all-powerful clergy to ban these scot-free revels.

Taken down a peg or two – to humble someone who has a high opinion of themselves. The beer connection comes from early medieval England when people drank beer from a communal vessel called a pottle. Shares of beer were measured with a peg slotted into a series of holes on the inside of the vessel. If someone drank more than they should the peg had to be moved down more than one space to try and even up the shares. This meant the rest of the people would get a short serving and be mad with the greedy drinker.

Getting plastered – meaning 'to be drunk'. Depending on the style of beer being brewed some brewers may add gypsum salts to the water to increase calcium sulphate levels. This enhances the flavour of the beer and improves the brewing process. Gypsum is used by builders to make plasterboard and by hospitals to make plaster of Paris for setting broken bones.

The following terms have several theories to their etymology and no one knows which one is correct – these are the ones associated with beer:

Mind your Ps and Qs – this means 'being on best behaviour'. A publican would warn rowdy customers to watch their Ps and Qs, meaning they should settle down and not knock over their pints and quarts.

Gone for a Burton – this means 'to have an accident or die'. Military personnel used it in the Second World War when one of their colleagues had 'bought it'. It was a euphemism for having disappeared to the pub for a pint of Burton ale.

Rule of thumb – before brewers had thermometers to measure the temperature of the brew to ensure it was just right for pitching in the yeast to start the fermentation, he or she would stick their thumb in the brew and make an educated guess.

CHIN CHIN – WORDS FOR CHEERS

When travelling overseas the essential phrases to learn are please, thank you, how to order to a drink, and bottoms up. Here is a lexicon of 'cheers', 'hair on your chest', or 'dry the glass' to help you on your way.

A votre santé (French)

Chok dee krap (Thai)

Egészségedre (Hungarian)

Gezondheid (Dutch)

Gëzuar (Albanian)

Iechyd da (Welsh)

Kanpai (Japanese)

Kippis (Finnish)

L'chaim (Hebrew)

Na zdorovye (Russian)

Na zdrowie (Polish)

Prost (German)

Salud (Spanish)

Salute (Italian)

Skål (Swedish and Norwegian)

Sláinte (Gaelic)

Ziveli (Serbian)

CLASSICAL DICTIONARY OF THE VULGAR TONGUE

Francis Grose's *Classical Dictionary of the Vulgar Tongue* was first published in 1785. Grose and his friend Tom Cocking spent nights walking through London docks, drinking dens, and slums making notes of slang words they overheard. In the nineteenth century *The Vulgar Tongue* was considered to be one of the most important collections of slang in the English language. These terms relate to alcohol and drinking.

DRINK

Barley Broth – strong beer

Dram-a-Tick – a drink served on credit

French Cream – brandy, so-called because dowagers added it to their tea

Gun – he is in the gun (he is drunk), reference to vessels called 'guns'

Hob or Nob? – warm or cold beer? Hob is warmed with a poker, nob is room temperature

Huckle My Buff – warm ale, brandy, and egg

Humpty Dumpty – warm ale and brandy

Kill Priest – port

Knock Me Down – old stingo (strong old ale)

Nappy Ale – strong ale

Pug Drink – watered-down cider

PART OF THE FURNITURE

Purl Royal – canary (wine) with wormwood

Purl – warm ale with wormwood

Red Tape – brandy

Six and Tips – whisky and small beer

Taplash – thick, sour beer

Whet – a morning draught, usually white wine

VESSELS

Dead Men – empty bottles

Magnum Bonum – 2 quarts of wine in a bottle

Marine Officer – empty bottle

Nip/Nyp – half pint of ale (from nipperkin, a small vessel)

Scotch Pint – bottle containing 2 quarts

Size of Ale – half a pint

Snout – a hogshead (in Grose's time this would have held about 54 gallons of beer)

Tallboy – a 2 quart pot or bottle

MISCELLANEOUS

Horse Meal – a meal without alcohol

Master of the Wardrobe – a man who pawns his clothes to buy alcohol

Mop Up – to drink up

Neck Stamper – a potboy who returns tankards used in private establishments back to the alehouse

Suck a Monkey – to suck alcohol out of a cask with a straw or tube

CHAPTER THREE:

RAISE A GLASS TO THE ANCESTORS

MESOPOTAMIA

'I feel wonderful drinking beer in a blissful mood with joy in my heart and a happy liver.' Who agrees with that tribute written by an unknown Sumerian poet around 5,000 years ago?

Sumer was an ancient culture in southern Mesopotamia – the land between the Tigris and Euphrates river systems that roughly corresponds with modern Iraq, Syria, Turkey and parts of Iran. This area of the world is called the Fertile Crescent, also known as the 'cradle of civilisation'. Nomadic tribes started to settle in one place, build irrigation ditches, plant crops and watch them grow rather than eat wild food on the move. And what were they growing? Barley, emmer, and wheat for making beer and bread.

So far, the earliest chemically analysed evidence of beer was discovered as a deposit on a clay jug at an archaeological site called Godin Tepe in the Zagros mountains of Iran. It dates back to around 3500 BC. Godin Tepe was a trading post along the Great Khorasan Road along which goods and people travelled from east to west. Beer may have been brewed thousands of years prior to this discovery but the proof has not yet been found. This region is also where the oldest confirmation of wine was found in a Neolithic village called Hajji Firuz Tepe built between 5400 and 5000 BC. Wild grapes probably grew in the area. Chemical analysis of pottery revealed residue of wine to which resin from the terebinth tree (from where we get the word 'turpentine') had been added for its antimicrobial properties to prevent the wine from spoiling, and possibly for its medicinal ability to treat internal ailments.

Beer was a staple in Sumerian society and brewing was a respectable profession for women and men. Additionally women were usually the innkeepers. As well as being highly nutritious, beer was a social drink as illustrated by an image on a cylinder seal discovered at Tepe Gawa in Iraq dating to around 3850 BC. Two figures are depicted sipping from a huge jar through drinking straws. Communal drinking is a recurring motif on Mesopotamian seals including ones found in the tomb of Queen Pu-abi at Ur dating from around

Such was the importance of beer in Sumerian society that daily rations were legally assigned. Free labourers usually received two crocks (approximately two gallons) per day. For civil servants and priestesses it was three crocks. But higher status members of society claimed five crocks a day. On religious feasts these rations were increased. All the better to worship the gods with.

RAISE A GLASS TO THE ANCESTORS

In Babylonia after a couple were married it was tradition for the bride's father to supply the newlyweds with a month's supply of honey beer or mead. Ninkasi was the goddess of fertility as well as beer so drinking her sacred liquid would no doubt enhance the chance of pregnancy. In that era time was measured by a lunar calendar and it took one month for the moon to orbit the earth – hence the term 'honeymoon' or 'honey-month' for the period after the nuptials.

Drinking straws were used for a practical reason – beer and wine was not filtered and so it would have had husks, pips and stalks floating around. A straw ensured the drinker could sip without ending up with a mouthful of detritus. Most people used the hollow stalks of plants such as reeds but upper-class Sumerians had ornate straws especially made in gold and lapis lazuli. And because beer and wine were also to be consumed in the after-life, their favourite decorated straw would go with them into the tomb.

'Hymn to Ninkasi', a poem that glorified the goddess Ninkasi, was written about 1800 BC. It is a recipe for beer. It was translated in 1964 by Professor of Sumerology Miguel Civil. This is one of the verses:

When you pour out the filtered beer of the collector vat
It is [like] the onrush of Tigris and Euphrates
Ninkasi, you are the one who pours out the filtered beer of the collector vat
It is [like] the onrush of Tigris and Euphrates

From: 'A hymn to the beer goddess and a drinking song', in *Studies Presented to A. Leo Oppenheim* (Chicago Oriental Institute, 1964)

2600 BC where guests at a banquet are enjoying shared crocks of beer and wine. Pu-abi's vault also contained hundreds of gold and silver goblets and lapis lazuli drinking straws so all that lovely drink could be enjoyed in the after-life.

Beer was proof of enlightenment, so much so that in the *Epic of Gilgamesh* (the world's earliest great work of literature, written in the eighteenth century BC) one of the characters, a naked wild man called Enkidu, is only fully human once he has consumed beer (and had a wash). Beer was enjoyed by everyone in Sumerian and later Babylonian society. Wine was popular too but just as in ancient Egypt it was restricted to the elite. It was imported at great expense from trading cultures such as the Phoenicians and the rarity value made wine the prestigious potation that Pushu-ken Public had no access to.

Beer was a sacred libation, a gift from the gods. One of the most important deities was Ninkasi, goddess of fertility, the harvest, seduction, and beer. She was the source of pleasure and her mortal acolytes drank in her name uttering *'Ninkasira'* as a toast. If Sumerians were not the world's original brewers, they were the earliest documented brewers because in this society written language developed. The first known recipe was written in cuneiform on clay tablets. It is a poem called 'The Hymn to Ninkasi' written about 1800 BC (see page 63) and includes instructions on how to make beer. In order to commune with the gods plentiful beer had to be consumed and sacrifice offered at the temple. Great public feasts where intoxication and loss of inhibitions was the aim created community bonds. To ensure supplies did not run out the temples housed breweries run by priestesses who also brewed the beer. In Sumer a range of beers described as red beer, dark beer, sweet dark beer, and golden beer were brewed. Hops were not known at that time so a variety of herbs, spices, fruits, and honey would have been added for flavour.

As the power of city state Babylon increased, Sumer gradually disappeared as a distinct culture. Beer remained the everyday drink for all and of such importance that regulations concerning its production and sale were included in the Code of Hammurabi written circa 1772 BC and named after the king. It is the oldest collection of written laws yet discovered and they are etched into a stone slab now on display in the Louvre museum, Paris. In comparison to Sumer's happy-go-lucky society, Babylon was strict. Rules relating to beer and brewing classified twenty styles including wheat, black, emmer and red. When it came to women and beer in Babylonia, female brewers and tavern keepers were disdained, unlike their male counterparts who were highly esteemed. The Code of Hammurabi decreed that any female brewer or tavern keeper who adulterated her beer or overcharged was to be drowned in it, for spoiled beer she would be force-fed with it until death by asphyxiation. And if customers discussed politics or anything subversive then the landlady would be executed. Priestesses who even visited a tavern, never mind ordered a pint, were to be burned alive on a pyre.

Mesopotamia was a land of perpetual change where one-time powerful cultures did not endure and throughout the millennia attitudes altered and with them drinking habits. Islam has been the dominant religion of the region since the seventh century AD, and that means alcohol is forbidden. What would Ninkasi think?

ANCIENT EGYPT

'The mouth of a perfectly contented man is filled with beer'. No, not a slogan for a modern brewery but an Egyptian inscription that dates back to 2200 BC.

Excavation of a site near Hierakonpolis suggests that beer was brewed in Egypt from at least 3400 BC. Brewing skills were most likely learned from history's first known brewers – the Sumerians (modern Iraq/Iran). As in Sumer ancient Egyptians understood beer to have divine origins and it featured in prayers and myths.

Beer was central to life in Egypt where it was regarded as food and consumed on a daily basis by adults and children. The hieroglyph for 'meal' is a compound of those for bread and beer. Add some dried fish and onions and you have the standard diet of countless people along the river Nile. Analysis of Egyptian texts discovered that the word for beer, *hekt*, was mentioned more often than any other foodstuff. Much is known about Egyptian culture because they were super-documentarians and left behind evidence of everyday life in hieroglyphs, murals, and tombs. Visitors to New York's Metropolitan Museum can look at effects from the tomb of a senior bureaucrat called Meketre who died in 1975 BC. Miniature carved wooden figures including bakers, cooks, carpenters and brewers represent Egyptians at work. In the mini-brewery two women grind flour, a man kneads it into dough, another figure treads the doughy mash with water in a tall vat, and then it is poured into crocks to ferment. After fermentation, it is transferred into round jugs sealed with clay stoppers. This is a hand-made model that demonstrates today how vital beer was almost 4,000 years ago.

Beer permeated every aspect of society as currency, medicine, religious observance. Some wages were paid in grain to make bread and beer. Beer was not just essential for the living, it was also required by the dead; a stash of beer was placed in tombs to be consumed in the after-life. Before sealing the mummified body into a vault, a ritual known as 'Opening the Mouth' was enacted where beer was poured into the mouth of the deceased to send them off to eternity.

Brewing was a state monopoly with strict rules to ensure supply and quality. Possibly the best job in the land was that of the royal chief beer inspector. Beer was made from barley and emmer with added ingredients for flavour such as dates, honey, spices. A variety of beer was brewed with varying strengths, colours, purposes or occasions for drinking and bestowed with poetic names such as 'beer of the protector', 'friends' beer', 'beer of truth'. All strata of society from slaves to the pharaoh were entitled by law to a daily ration of beer – the higher the status the more they received.

As beer was used in religious worship many temples operated breweries and pubs in the service of the gods. Intoxication in everyday life was usually condemned but religious holidays were joyous occasions that incorporated much drinking. An inscription from the fourth century BC tomb of Petosiris reads 'Drink till drunk while enjoying the feast day!' Affluent Egyptians would be accompanied by two slaves and a hammock in order to be carried home when they were legless.

People of wealth lived it up at banquets whereas the lower classes frequented inns and beer halls where singing, dancing, and gambling accompanied the liberal consumption of drinks into the late hours. Both sexes were free to interact with each other, although respectable women would not be seen in such places – if they wanted a tipple they did it at home.

If beer was the drink of one and all in ancient Egypt, wine was reserved for the ruling classes. Wild grapes had never grown in Egypt so until a royal winemaking industry started in the Nile Delta around 3000 BC wine was imported from the Levant where domesticated vines grew. Wine could be made from locally grown fruits such as dates and pomegranates, and sap from palm trees, flavoured with herbs and spices but grape wine had all the status and it played a major ceremonial role, particularly in the temple. A royal sealer of wine was appointed to guarantee honest labelling of wine amphorae. As with modern wine labels, those in ancient Egypt recorded the name of the estate, location, type of wine, date of vintage, vintner's name, and quality. Amongst the most-celebrated vineyards were Phoenix Estate, Star of Horus on the Height of Heaven, and the Preserver of Kemet. By 2200 BC wine was the essential oblation at major religious festivals including one called *heb-sed* to ensure the health of the pharaoh and the fruitfulness of the earth. This demanded prodigious drinking and offerings to the gods and could last for weeks.

If wine was good enough for the living, it certainly was for the dead. The deceased could rest for eternity knowing that only the best vino had been stored in their tombs. Residue on five of the twenty-six wine amphorae discovered in the tomb of Tutankhamun (1323 BC) was analysed and found to be the highest-quality Shedeh (red wine), the

Sicilian historian Diodorus Siculus (c.90–21 BC) wrote of beer in *Bibliotheca Historica*, his history of the world: 'They make a drink from barley in Egypt, which is called zytum, and it compares not unfavourably in pleasantness of colour and taste to wine'.

Scorpion I, one of the first kings of Egypt, reigned around 3150 BC. Archaeologists who excavated his magnificent tomb at Abydos discovered a vast supply of food and drink to ensure he did not go without in the after-life. The stash included 700 clay jars containing approximately 4500 litres of resinated wine.

'In water you see your own face, but in wine the heart of its garden.'
Ancient Egyptian proverb

In one ancient Egyptian text a teacher wrote to an errant student: 'I hear that you are neglecting your writing and spending all your time dancing, going from tavern to tavern always reeking of beer. If only you realised that wine is a thing of the Devil. You sit in front of the wench, sprinkled with perfume, your garland hangs around your neck and you drum on your paunch, you reel and fall on your belly and are anointed with dirt.' Little has changed in student behaviour over millennia, has it?

most precious drink of the time in Egypt. In case the departed needed a reminder of what fun beer and wine was, murals depicting scenes of drinking were painted on tomb walls. In the grave of Peheri dating from circa 1425 BC a high-status woman presents an empty cup to her servant and says: 'Give me eighteen measures of wine. Behold I should love to drink to drunkenness.'

Beer continued to be consumed by almost everyone, rich and poor, but after the country came under Greek rule from 332 BC, contemporary written references to beer became rare. Nevertheless its reputation as being one of the major beer cultures of antiquity is sealed because if you ask people where in the world beer was first consumed, a majority will answer Egypt.

ANCIENT GREECE

Wine drinkers of the world thank the ancient Greeks and a culture so desirable to the Romans that they emulated it. A combination of colonisation and trade by Greece and later Rome spread viticulture far and wide. Yes the Romans were consumed with oeno-passion but they were copying the oh-so sophisticated Greeks with their *oinos* (wine).

To the Hellenes, wine was not just an agreeable potation it was also currency, medicine, and an offering to the deities. Oaths and contracts sealed with wine had greater magnitude than ones sealed with water. Wine bound society together at public feasts, was an emblem of superior intellect, and a sign of civilisation that separated the Greeks from the dreadful non-wine drinking *barbaroi* in the rest of the world. Dionysus, the god of wine, had bestowed the precious gift upon the deserving Hellenes when he presented a goat herder with vines and explained how to cultivate them and make wine. Greeks drank wine resinated with gum from the terebinth tree. This was a preservative that slowed oxidation and prevented wine turning to vinegar. Seawater, spices, and honey were also often added for flavour.

Greece may have learned viticulture through trade with Egypt and Canaan (the Levant). Wine reached the Hellenic peninsula around 2000 BC. Beer was already known to the people of that area and so was mead. Those two drinks combined with wine made a widely consumed grog called *kykeon*. Elaborately decorated chalices, stirrup jars, and spouted drinking horns have been found which prove that it was popular enough to warrant the expense of special drinking vessels. A gold cup from a sixteenth-century BC royal grave suggests that higher status people drank *kykeon* too.

Wine drinking by the elite in social, secular and sacred rituals elevated its position. When philosophers, playwrights and poets started to rhapsodise about wine it became fixed as the aspirational drink that cultured people consumed and in most wine-drinking societies from then on that was and still is the case.

Greeks had conflicting attitudes to beer. Some considered it to be a foul-smelling, wind-causing beverage of the 'other' (i.e. foreigners) and was only to be consumed when wine was not available; whilst others thought it was a divine gift, nutritious and healthful. Sophocles believed that the most wholesome diet consisted of bread, meats, vegetables, and beer (*zythos*).

Social wine drinking was undertaken according to strict rules. Tradition in Athens dictated that three libations were poured to honour the deities, fallen heroes, and Zeus (father of the gods). Men gathered at formal drinking parties called symposia – from the Greek word *sympotein* meaning drinking party – in a room called the *andron* (the male quarters of the household) where guests reclined on sofas. Women were forbidden to attend these gatherings. Symposia were banquets followed by ritual wine drinking. The group would decide beforehand how many *kraters* (vessels the size of garden urns) of wine were to be consumed. Wine was poured into decorated drinking bowls and water added from a *hydria* – Greeks always watered their wine, only barbarians and drunkards would want it neat. Music, singing, poetry was the entertainment and then the men got down to the serious business of conversation, debate, showing off, joke telling, carousing, and drinking games such as *kottabus* which involved flicking droplets of wine at a floating target with the intention of sinking it. Plato suggested that youths should attend symposia to learn the rituals of drinking wine so they could understand the effects of intoxication and learn discipline in drinking.

Early Greeks had a reputation for drinking in moderation but people did let go and get drunk especially during adoration of the gods. It was believed they would not listen unless worshippers were on the lash. Being intoxicated was no social faux pas as drinking wine was a civilised activity that helped people to relax, inspired wisdom, and enhanced the art of oratory which was highly valued. People who chose sobriety were considered to be outside of social norms. This is often still the case today – 'oh, go on, just have one' being a refrain familiar to people who choose not to drink. Drinking is a social activity and generally people want everyone in the group to be in the same altered state.

Women in ancient Greece were discouraged, although not forbidden, from drinking. Wine was believed to make them violent. Women had to be secret drinkers and discreetly visit taverns (*kapelion*) rather than do it at home where the key to the drinks cabinet was held by the house slave. The exception was during the worship of the gods when it was essential to lose inhibitions. Many females embraced the cult of Dionysus which was a good excuse to drink lots of wine in the veneration of one of the most important deities – a son of Zeus. Dionysus (who was renamed Bacchus by the Romans) was known as the liberator who led his followers into states of ecstasy. No wonder he was such a popular deity.

ANCIENT ROME

What beer was to ancient Egypt, wine was to the Romans – an essential for life. Beer was consumed but normally only when wine was not available. Initially wine was restricted to the elite and people drank modestly but eventually it became ubiquitous in all strata of Roman society of drinking age (thirty years and older) no matter what the person's status. Even slaves drank wine, although it was low quality and had only a passing acquaintance with grape juice. Wine was the egalitarian beverage – if you were a man. For women it was unacceptable, and in the early years of the Roman era even forbidden, to drink wine. Women who fancied a drinkie had to be clandestine. Consequently the stereotype of the female tippler appeared regularly in jokes and comedy plays as someone out of control and indulging in vice. Later in the Roman age women could drink and even attend a *convivium*. These were based on the Greek *symposium* but the Roman version was more ostentatious and concerned with having a knees-up rather than the formal drinking party of their Hellenic counterparts where females were excluded and the amount of wine was rationed.

Wine culture came to the Romans from the Greeks and the Etruscans (who lived in the area around Tuscany and western Umbria) and they embraced it with gusto. To the Romans, wine equalled civilisation. Wine was initially imported from Greece and its territories in what is now southern Italy and Sicily as Romans were not skilled in viticulture. But demand escalated with the spread of Roman power, not least because legionnaires in an increasingly large army required a daily wine ration to maintain morale. The empire could no longer rely on imports – a home-grown wine industry was required. Triumph over Carthage in the Punic Wars (264–146 BC) gave the Romans access to extensive written works on viticulture from ransacked libraries. They were translated by Marcus Porcius Cato into a work called *De Agri Cultura* (*On Agriculture*) which is the earliest surviving work of Latin prose. With this knowledge the Romans began to classify grape varieties, identify diseases, research soil-type preferences, and introduce irrigation and fertilisation techniques. He wrote that slaves should have one gallon of wine per week as their ration. This was not for pleasure but for the sake of maintaining their strength and dietary health. If illness prevented a slave from working, Cato advised halving the rations to conserve wine for the healthy slaves.

Eventually the Romans were the world's experts in viticulture and planted vines in lands they occupied including France, Portugal, Germany, and Spain. Wine was highly sought after and such a luxury item to Gauls (Celtic inhabitants of Western Europe) and so prized that the elite would exchange one slave for a jar of wine. Once the Gauls had embraced wine, the Romans considered them to be civilised.

Like the Greeks whom they emulated in all things oeno (wine passion), Romans poured water, sometimes seawater, into their wine before consuming it. They also added herbs and spices to make *conditum*, honey to make *mulsum*, and resins such as frankincense and myrrh to preserve the wine. *Mulsum* was handed out to the masses at public events as bribes to solicit political support.

The Roman equivalent of the pub was the *taberna* which served red wine, occasionally beer, food and a luxury – hot water considered to have medicinal properties that restored bodily equilibrium. Typically *tabernae* consisted of one large room with a counter behind which wine *amphorae* were stored. Music, singing, dancing, competitive drinking bouts, saucy behaviour and gambling were normal conduct in *tabernae*. Dice and four-sided knuckle bones were thrown to gamble with, and bets were laid on cockfights. Just as in a British pub, a *taberna* served an important social function where community bonds were built in a neutral setting when people of different classes could hob-nob. They were largely male domains as it was not socially acceptable for respectable women to frequent such establishments. Women who did were either lower class, or prostitutes.

White wine was reserved for the elite and the most esteemed was *Falernian* which improved after years of maturation. It was reputed to be high enough in alcohol (around 15 per cent ABV) for Pliny the Elder to note that 'it is the only wine that takes light when a flame is applied to it'. It was also the wine (vintage 121 BC) served at a banquet in 60 BC to honour Julius Caesar for his conquests in Spain. The least desirable wine was *lora* made by soaking in water the skins, pips and stalks of grapes that had already been pressed twice and then fermenting it. *Lora* was an unappetising coarse and bitter tannic draft consumed by slaves and the poor. Slightly above *lora* in quality was *posca* – a low alcohol mixture of sour wine and water. This was the usual wine for soldiers' rations and approximately one litre a day was codified in the *Corpus Juris Civilis*. Woe betide the powers that be if they failed to ensure a wine ration for men who maintained the security of the empire.

Pompeii was one of the most important centres for wine in the Roman Empire both in producing and trading. *Amphorae* bearing the emblems of Pompeii have been found as far north as Toulouse in France and as far west as Spain. Surrounding the town were some of the best vineyards in the world. Most wine consumed in the city of Rome came from that region. Pompeii was also a lively social centre with approximately 200 *tabernae* and *thermopolia* (snack bars) all selling wine from *amphorae* stored on racks and decanted into carafes. When Vesuvius erupted in AD 79 not only was it a human tragedy but vineyards and wine warehouses were wrecked. This led to severe shortages and a dramatic price rise so that only the wealthy could afford wine. Panic set in and vines were planted anywhere suitable, including in what had previously been grain fields. It was not long before there was a scarcity of grain and a glut of grapes. This wine lake spurred Emperor Domitian to release an edict to ban the planting of new vineyards in Italy and the removal of half the vines in the provinces. But the genie was out of the wine bottle and viticulture had become embedded in the countries of the empire and the psyche of the peoples of lived there. Wine was part of their identity.

Next time the question 'What did the Romans do for us?' is asked, one of the answers is sitting in that bottle of Viognier on the shelf. The influence of Rome is still apparent in today's wine industry.

Roman soldiers stationed in Britain drank beer as well as wine. Beer was mentioned in writing on a number of wooden tablets found at the Vindolanda fort on Hadrian's Wall. In a message sent around AD 100 the decurion Masculus wrote to the fort's prefect Flavius Cerialis: 'Please my lord, give instructions on what you want us to do tomorrow. Are we to return with the standard, or just half of us [missing lines]… My fellow soldiers have no beer. Please order some to be sent.' The local brewer was called Atrectus and he would have made his beer from locally grown cereal. This is the earliest documented name of a British brewer.

In the early centuries of the Roman era when women were forbidden to drink wine in day-to-day life they were often the most enthusiastic participants in the cult of Bacchus when the god of wine was venerated with intoxicated frenzy. In 186 BC such worship was outlawed by the senate and men were legally allowed to divorce or even kill their wives if they were caught drinking too much wine. The last-known divorce for Bacchus adulation was recorded in 194 BC and from then on attitudes to women drinking wine became more tolerant as it was considered to be a dietary staple.

Although vines were planted in Britain by the Romans, they probably yielded few grapes. Instead the Romans imported wine. Excavations in Colchester, one-time capital of Roman Britain, uncovered containers of over sixty different types of wines from Italy, Spain, the Rhine and Bordeaux. Some Britons enthusiastically embraced the cult of Bacchus, where the Roman god of wine was worshipped with wild revels. Hundreds of artefacts bearing his likeness have been found throughout Britain. When in Rome, do as the Romans do.

CHAPTER FOUR:

THE SHOPPING LIST

POPPING THE CORK

Cork is sourced from living bark tissue of a species of oak called *Quercus suber* (the cork oak) which grows in Southern Europe (principally Spain, Portugal and Italy) and in North Africa. In Europe, corks did not become widely used until the end of the seventeenth century. Before this, bottles were closed by stuffing their ends with cloths, pieces of wood, or pebbles. The impermeability and elasticity of cork makes it a perfect material because when inserted into the bottle neck it expands to form an airtight seal.

No trees are harmed in the harvesting of the bark and it is done in spring and summer by experts called 'extractors' when the tree is in full growth and the bark is loose on the trunk. A cork tree has a life span of up to 250 years and stripping the bark is done only once every nine to twelve years in order to maintain the health of the tree. The bark is cut into planks which are sent to the cork factory, boiled in water to soften and clean them before they are hand-punched into corks for high-quality wines. For less expensive wines the planks are machine-punched.

A wine described as 'corked' does not have fragments of cork floating in it, rather the wine has a musty smell usually caused by contamination by the chemical compound TCA (2,4,6-Trichloroanisole). This is usually caused when airborne fungi are in contact with chlorophenols which then convert to chloroanisole and adversely affect the aroma and taste of the wine. Ironically chlorophenols may result from the very process used to sterilise corks. Buyers do not know a wine is corked until they open the bottle and this lottery has led to the increasing adoption of screw caps or synthetic stoppers made from plastic. Some wine lovers reluctantly accept the modern closures but prefer the tradition of cork.

What good is a cork if it cannot be removed? Cue the corkscrew, possibly invented in England in the mid-seventeenth century. Bottle screws (as they were initially known) were first patented in 1795 by an English cleric, Reverend Samuel Henshall. Original straight-pull Henshall corkscrews can be identified by an inscription 'Obstando promoves, Soho Patent'. The Latin phrase loosely translates as 'by standing firm one moves forward' and Soho Patent refers to the place of manufacture at Matthew Boulton's metal works in Birmingham.

Undisputed cork champion is the Whistler Tree in Portugal's Alentejo region. At fourteen metres high and with a circumference of more than four metres it is the world's largest and most productive cork oak tree. When last harvested it produced almost one ton of cork – twelve times the yield of an average cork oak. This was enough for almost 100,000 wine bottles. Named for the dozens of songbirds that roost in its canopy, it has been producing the finest quality wine corks every nine years since 1820.

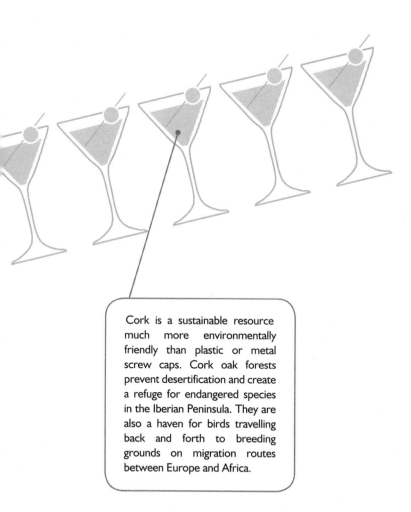

Cork is a sustainable resource much more environmentally friendly than plastic or metal screw caps. Cork oak forests prevent desertification and create a refuge for endangered species in the Iberian Peninsula. They are also a haven for birds travelling back and forth to breeding grounds on migration routes between Europe and Africa.

WOLF PLANT – HOPS

If you have ever wondered what beer made without hops would taste like, dilute Ovaltine in water. Ovaltine is made from malted cereal (with added sugar) and is similar in taste to the wort produced in a brewery during the malt-mashing process, i.e. sweet. It is the addition of hops that add bitterness to beer.

Hops are perennial herbaceous climbing plants that grow by winding around wires strung across poles in hop gardens. In Latin they are known as *Humulus lupulus* which translates roughly as 'wolf plant'. It belongs to the *Cannabaceae* family which also includes cannabis although the compound tetrahydrocannabinol (THC) that delivers psychotropic effects is not present in hops. For a buzz drink the hops in beer rather than smoking them!

Hops grow in temperate climates such as Germany, Czech Republic, USA, Australia, and New Zealand. In Britain the main cultivating regions are Worcestershire, Herefordshire and Kent. Nowadays hops are primarily used for beer but the shoots are edible, tasty and known as 'poor man's asparagus' although it is much easier to buy a bunch of asparagus than hop shoots as they are not commercially harvested.

Brewers use female hop flowers because they produce yellow powder called lupulin containing resin in which alpha and beta acids and essential oils are concentrated. Male flowers contain a fraction of the active ingredients hence the reason for using the females.

Hops give bitterness, aroma and flavour to beer, and they are also a natural preservative with antibacterial properties. Think of hops as the brewer's herbs and spices. Depending on varietal, the character they impart to beer might be floral, citrus, grassy, fruity, herbal, woody, spicy, peppery, or earthy. Some people sigh at the very names of hops and consider them poetry – Pacific Jade, Cascade, Challenger, Goldings, Fuggles, Galaxy. The style of beer will determine which type of hops are used so in an India Pale Ale the hops will be highly aromatic and bitter, whereas in pilsener lager the hops will give bitterness but little aroma.

Most commercially produced beer now contains hops but in the lengthy historic timeframe of brewing their inclusion is a recent innovation. Hops were first documented in connection with beer in AD 822 at a Benedictine monastery in France. Around 1150 in Germany, St Hildegard of Bingen, nun, composer, philosopher and healer highlighted hops in her book *Physica Sacra* when she wrote 'as a result of its own bitterness it keeps some putrefactions from drinks, to which it may be added, so that they may last so much longer'. Thanks to the blessed Hildegarde, brewers had found in hops the Holy Grail – a natural preservative.

Commercial hop cultivation is thought to have started in Northern Germany in the twelfth or thirteenth century. German beers were widely traded and the reputation of hopped beers grew. As demand for hopped beer spread into other countries so did cultivation and now hops are grown across the world. But it is rather appropriate that even today the world's biggest continuous hop-growing region is in Germany – Hallertau, Bavaria.

Brewer's droop is a real condition triggered by a compound in hops. They contain a herbal form of the female hormone oestrogen which can cause erectile dysfunction. Alcohol is an anaphrodisiac in men, i.e. it represses libido by depressing nerve centres in the hypothalamus and the release of sex hormones. So although the beer goggles phenomenon certainly exists it may be a case of wishful thinking. Shakespeare referred to brewer's droop in *Macbeth* (Act II, scene iii) when Macduff says to the porter: 'What three things does drink especially promote?'

The porter replies: 'Marry, sir, nose-painting, sleep, and urine. Lechery, sir, it provokes, and unprovokes; it provokes the desire, but it takes away the performance. Therefore much drink may be said to be an equivocator with lechery. It makes him, and mars him; it sets him on, and it takes him off; it persuades him, and disheartens him; makes him stand to and not to stand to; in conclusion, equivocates him in a sleep and giving him the lie, leaves him.'

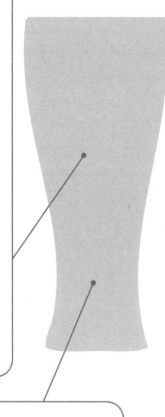

Hops are used in natural medicine to treat a variety of ailments including insomnia, tension, irritability, indigestion, intestinal cramps, to purify blood, stimulate a sluggish liver, and externally to reduce swelling, and treat skin irritation.

Hopping down to Kent. This describes the annual hop harvest when casual labour flocked to pick hops in Kent (and other counties). Generations of families (even small children) would be involved in picking. In Kent, pickers usually came from poor areas of the East End of London and quite often the menfolk would work in London during the week and then visit their families at weekends staying with them in basic communal accommodation in the hop gardens. Sometimes described as a 'working holiday' hop picking was hard toil but it was a chance for urban people to spend a few weeks in the fresh air. Since the 1960s, most hops have been machine picked and humans are no longer required.

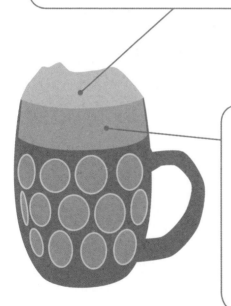

Beer drinkers often need the loo. Blame all that water – a pint of beer is over 90 per cent H_2O, but hops are culprits too. They are diuretic and stimulate the kidneys. That's the irony of drinking beer – all that water yet drinkers can end up dehydrated.

In the early twentieth century when telephone exchanges were assigned three letters to identify them, Southwark in south London was HOP. It was the pre-eminent hop marketing quarter due to its proximity to London Bridge and location on the main road to Kent where most hops were grown. When the railways came, London Bridge station was the main destination for hops from the Garden of England.

Some brewers use fresh hops, i.e. straight off the bine. They are rushed to the brewery within hours of picking and used to brew a style called green hop beer.

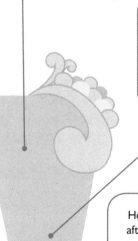

Hops are dried as soon as possible after harvest to prevent them from turning mouldy. Those distinctive conical roofed buildings widely seen in Kent are called oast houses – large kilns used to dry hops.

MARVELLOUS MALT

Malt, the backbone of beer and distilled spirits such as whisky, is a term used to describe barley or whatever grain the brewers and distillers use in their craft. They need a source of starch and that comes from the cereal. Without sugar there will be no alcohol. Yeast consumes sugar during fermentation and the by-product is alcohol and carbon dioxide.

Malt goes through the malting process in which the cereal is steeped in water to initiate germination. This procedure develops the enzymes that will later convert starch to sugars. To halt germination the cereal is heated, toasted or roasted and depending on the temperature this will change the colour and flavour. With beer malt provides colour and flavour and brewers use a variety ranging from pale, amber, crystal, chocolate, brown and black. Whisky distillers, however, use only pale malts – and the colour of whisky comes from being in contact with wood during maturation in oak barrels. Flavours from malt depending on toasting or roasting include biscuit, grain, sweetcorn, caramel, smoke, coffee, and chocolate.

During a process called 'mashing' when hot water is sprayed through the malt to become a liquid called wort, enzymes convert the starch to simple fermentable sugars including maltose. Barley has high enzyme content and that is why it is the preferred choice for brewing. Even a wheat beer will contain a large percentage of barley malt. After the wort is brewed and cooled it is transferred to a vessel where yeast is added and fermentation commences. The yeast ferments the sugars in the brew to supply alcohol. Magic malt.

Anything that contains starch can be used to make beer. Barley is the best cereal to use but in cultures where beer is still made in the home and where barley may not grow, local ingredients are used. In Africa these might be banana, or sorghum; in the Amazon forest it is corn or cassava. The question is how to change the starch to sugar when the nearest maltster is thousands of miles away? No problem, just chew whatever starchy food is being used and the enzymes in saliva will magically transform the starch to sugars. Spit it out, form into a small ball to dry in the sun, then add water, boil, cool, and leave it to ferment and turn into beer.

Shakespeare used the term 'malt worm', sixteenth-century slang for a beer tippler, in at least two of his plays. In *Henry IV Part I* Gadshill says: *'I am joined with no foot-land rakers, no long-staff sixpenny strikers, none of these mad mustachio purple hued malt worms'*.

As the colour of malt determines the shade of beer, historically the fuel used for malting cereal was significant. Wood or straw that flared as it burned would roast and smoke the cereal leading to dark smoky beers. Coal was no use as it gave off noxious fumes which tainted the grain, but coke with the poisonous volatile elements removed gave off heat but no fumes and burned steadily so it was possible to create pale malts – hence the production of pale ales. In England the first documented evidence of pale malts was in Derbyshire around 1640 when maltsters started using the new fuel of coke. Until that point unless malt was sun-dried (not easy with Britain's climate!) most beers in Blighty were dark.

Why does beer have a frothy head? Because the malt contains proteins and these combine with hop compounds, yeast, and air bubbles. Wheat has more of the foam-enhancing proteins so wheat beers have naturally larger heads when poured.

GOD-IS-GOOD
– YEAST AND
FERMENTATION

Drinkers of the world, meet your best mates Saccharomyces cerevisiae and Saccharomyces bayanus for without them we would not have those marvellous fermented fruit and cereal sugars used to make alcoholic drinks. Our Latin-monikered friends are fungi – microscopic single-celled organisms that float around in the air with the sole intention of searching for sugar. Once found they go bonkers and start to reproduce by forming buds which then detach from the mother (asexual reproduction so female only, no male yeast). These daughters are clones and they too grow buds that separate so the mass of yeast cells grows, doubling in number in 90 minutes. In brewing and winemaking this growth is eventually visible to the naked eye and creates a seething foamy substance. This is where the word yeast originates – Old English *gyst* (also spelled *giest*) possibly from a Sanskrit word *yasati* meaning to foam, boil or bubble. Such magic was not fully understood until the nineteenth century when scientists Theodore Schwann and later Louis Pasteur and Emile Hansen studied yeast and fathomed what it was and its role in fermentation. For millennia it had been a mystery and in medieval England the lather that appeared in the beer, cider or wine vat was known as God-is-good and thought to be sent by a higher power. During Louis Pasteur's research into why

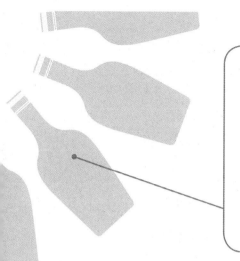

Yeast is everywhere – in the air, on the surface of inanimate objects, in the skin, hair, and digestive tracts of living organisms. Millions of spores live on the skin of fruit. Look at a grape and that bloom on the surface is yeast just waiting for the skin to deteriorate and expose the precious sugary juice.

some wine spoils his studies revealed that yeast sugars convert to alcohol and carbon dioxide. The investigation also revealed that bacterial contamination and certain wild yeasts could cause wine to go off. This led to the innovation that bears his name, pasteurisation, where a liquid is heated, usually to around 70 °C, to kill any spoilage organisms. Emile Hansen experimenting at the Carlsberg brewery in Copenhagen isolated hybrids of yeast which were very stable. That was beneficial for brewers as it meant the quality of beer improved.

If alcohol was not enough of a prize, yeast is also highly nutritious and contains proteins, essential minerals and vitamins – especially B vitamins – so although some people think Marmite (made from spent brewer's yeast) to be the spawn of the Devil, consider this. A pint of real ale with a plate of Marmite soldiers on the side supplies a variety of essential amino acids that the body cannot produce – so really we can't live without it.

Jurassic Park as a reality may not be too far-fetched and Cuban American microbiologist Dr Raul Cano can prove it. In 1995 he extracted the digestive tract contents of a bee encased in fossilised tree sap and placed the material in a warm nutritious solution. Within a week bacterial spores that had lain dormant inside the bee for between 25 million and 40 million years were revived.

Some of the organisms resembled *Saccharomyces cerevisiae* and Dr Cano wanted to find a commercial application for his Lazarus life form. Beer was the answer and together with a colleague he made some home-brew with the spores. It worked, so Cano approached a microbrewer from California to make a batch commercially. The result was a light copper ale with lemon and spice aroma. According to the brewer the yeast did not act as regular brewer's yeast does and at first created a violent fermentation, then sank to the bottom of the tank and languidly nibbled the sugar. Not surprising behaviour for an organism that had been trapped in amber for an eon.

Most commercial brewers use cultured yeasts. This way they can anticipate the yeast's behaviour during fermentation and the resulting aromas (esters) that become associated with the particular brand of beer. But some brewers want wild yeast such as *Brettanomyces* and other microflora to ferment the brew because the resulting beers are unpredictable. The best known example of this is the lambic beers of Belgium. They rely on spontaneous fermentation from airborne spores that live in the local atmosphere or the building structure of the brewery. Wild yeast imparts a sourness which can resemble vinegar. In most other beers of the world this would be a defect, but in lambics it is essential. Look out for styles called Flanders red, Flanders brown ale (a.k.a. *oud bruin*), and *gueuze*. Then prepare for a surprise – face-scrunchingly good for anyone partial to grapefruit juice. If not, persevere to the third mouthful because after the second the brain gets used to the unusual flavour and by the third it will say 'don't take away the bottle'.

Top and bottom fermenting yeast is a way of classifying beers into ales or lagers. It describes what is supposed to happen to the yeast during fermentation. With ales the yeast cells normally float to the top of the brew and with lagers they drop to the bottom. However, in reality it is not really accurate because some so-called top fermenting yeasts drop to the bottom of the vat. But it is widely used simple shorthand to differentiate between ales and lagers.

Fermentation is a spectacular phenomenon. Alcohol and carbon dioxide are waste products and that means they are toxic to the organism that produced them. Yeast must be hardy to survive the maelstrom and when alcohol levels start rising this spells trouble. Only the toughest yeast strains will survive in high alcohol conditions and there is therefore a limit to the level of alcohol produced by fermentation – up to 20 per cent ABV in exceptional circumstances. Wines such as port and sherry are fortified with distilled grape spirit for higher alcohol levels. Some of the gimmicky beers that claim to be the world's strongest at up to 40 per cent ABV or more do not achieve that by fermentation alone. For several weeks the brewer freezes the beer. Alcohol freezes at lower temperatures than water so by extracting ice (H_2O) from the solution the alcohol concentration remaining is increased.

A GHOSTLY WRAITH – DISTILLATION

Take two glasses – one of wine and one of brandy. The wine may be fruity and smooth, the brandy is likely to burn the roof off your mouth. Believe it or not they are versions of the same thing – fermented grape juice. But with the brandy the wine has been distilled. Whisky, gin, vodka, *eau de vie*, Tequila, ouzo, grappa, rum, anise, and all other distilled spirits start off as a benign sugary liquid and then end up as fire water.

Who were the first distillers? No one knows exactly but some academics believe that Chinese alchemists may have discovered the process of distillation in the first millennium BC and used it for making medicines. The ancient Greeks purified water by distilling it and one of the terms for a type of distilling jar, alembic, came from the Greek word for 'cup' *ambix* and entered the English language via the Arabic *al ambic*. Arab chemists experimented by distilling fruits and flower essences for perfumes and medicine. The word alcohol may derive from the Arabic word for a ghostly spirit *al ghūl* because that is what the steam created during distillation resembles. Like so much in the history of alcohol the skills and knowledge of distilling spread with trade, occupation, reputation. Distillation was introduced into Europe by the Moors, Arabs from North Africa, who occupied Spain from the early eighth century. From then on it was enthusiastically practised in Christian monasteries primarily to make medicinal elixirs for the preservation of health and the relief of specific ailments. Its properties as an antiseptic, painkiller, and water purifier earned it the name *aqua vitae* or *eau de vie* (water of life) and that enduring excuse for drinking – for medicinal purposes only.

No need for a spoonful of sugar to help the medicine go down. Consumption of alcoholic potions increased during the fourteenth century when the Black Death ravaged the population in so many European countries. They did not work as a preventative or cure but may have soothed the misery of those suffering from the plague by sending them into an *aqua vitae* haze.

Where grapes were not plentiful, distilled alcohol was made from cereals instead. Thus in Southern Europe the national distilled drinks – brandy, grappa, ouzo were made by distilling fermented grape juice; but in the colder climes of Northern Europe whisky, vodka, gin, genever, aquavit were made by distilling barley, corn or wheat.

HOW DISTILLATION WORKS

Depending on what spirit is being produced, grapes, apples, soft fruits, cereals, molasses, potatoes, or some other source of sugar are fermented. Alcohol is the by-product. Simple distillation is performed in a pot still (a.k.a. alembic) which consists of two flasks connected by a tube. In the first flask the fermented liquid is boiled so the water, alcohol and aroma compounds vaporise and accumulate in the tube where they condense on a cold serpentine coil. Condensate of concentrated alcohol trickles drop by drop into the second flask. The first run-off is called 'the head' and being low grade is discarded because the distiller is after 'the heart' which is the high-quality distillate in the middle of the process to be used as the final product. During distillation chemical reactions take place that change the aroma and flavour characteristics of the original fermented brew. The condensed liquid is a colourless spirit, so for drinks like whisky, rum and brandy it is aged in oak casks for several years and the wood imparts a golden amber hue, aroma and flavour. With gin, anise and flavoured vodka, the spirit is either distilled again or infused with botanicals to give the distinctive flavours.

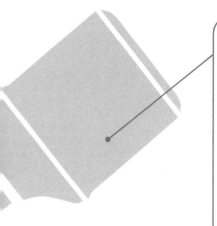

Schnapps (or schnaps) is a general term derived from the German word *schnaps* (meaning swallow) and is used to describe a range of spirits distilled from cereal, potatoes, fruit, or molasses. They can be flavoured with anything the distiller fancies. The difference between *eau de vie* and vodka is negligible, so do as the Germans do and use the term schnapps to describe any strong drink originating in northern European countries.

Norway has a unique distilled drink called Linie aquavit. It is produced in the same way as other aquavits but Linie has a distinctly different character thanks to something that happened in 1805. A cargo of aquavit stored in sherry barrels was shipped to Indonesia but failed to find a buyer and two years later it was returned to Norway. When sampled it was much smoother than regular aquavits. So since then to be called Linie, it must travel overseas in an oak barrel for a few months and cross the equator (the *linie*, or line) twice before heading home. During the voyage the spirit sloshes around on the high seas and the oak barrels swell and contract in the extremes of humidity. Something magical happens to improve the spirit with enhanced flavours. If this sounds far-fetched it isn't; scientists tried to replicate the effects of the journey with temperature changes, and by rocking the barrels, but they could not reproduce the character of the aquavit that had crossed the equator.

CHAPTER FIVE:

BEHIND THE BAR

THE EMERALD SORCERESS – ABSINTHE

Forbidden pleasure, hypnotic ecstasy – absinthe drinkers were so entranced with its spellbinding powers they bestowed nicknames such as Sorceress, *la Fée Verte* (green fairy), the White Witch. Has any drink in history had such a saucy reputation? Generally associated with the Bohemians of France's belle époque, absinthe was believed to stimulate creativity and its best-known devotees were artists and writers such as Van Gogh, Toulouse-Lautrec, and Baudelaire who professed it to be their muse.

Absinthe is an emerald-green aniseed-flavoured distilled spirit containing amongst other botanicals a bitter herb called wormwood. Its closest cousin is Pernod. Wormwood's Latin name *Artemisia absinthium* may derive from Artemis, the Greek goddess of the forest, fertility, and hunt who in mythology gave wormwood to a centaur named Chiron to use as medicine. Wormwood is extremely bitter and unpleasant to drink; champions at the ancient Olympics would down a potion of wine and wormwood as a reminder to remain humble in victory.

Like gin, absinthe was first taken as a general-purpose elixir. From at least the mid-eighteenth century it was prepared in the Swiss village of Couvet by infusing locally grown wormwood and other herbs in wine. When French physician Pierre Ordinaire moved to the area in 1792 he experimented with the local tincture and mixed the botanicals in distilled spirit. It became popular as a social drink and one of Dr Ordinaire's customers liked it so much he bought the recipe and founded a distillery in France with his son-in-law Henri-Louis Pernod to produce it on a commercial basis. Sales of absinthe grew when it was included in the rations of French soldiers. During their conquest of Algeria in 1830 it was used as a water purifier. From then on absinthe in France was a patriotic aperitif associated with military glory and the habit of drinking it spread to French-influenced communities around the world including Tahiti, Vietnam and New Orleans.

After the vine louse *Phylloxera vastatrix* devastated the French wine industry in the mid-nineteenth century and supplies of the national drink were restricted, drinking absinthe became a craze. Those partial to a drop or twenty were known as *absintheurs*, and doctors identified in heavy drinkers a syndrome called absinthism characterised by sleeplessness, tremors, convulsions, mental instability and hallucinations. The culprit, or so experts believed at the time, was wormwood which contained a compound called thujone and this was believed (erroneously) to have psychedelic properties. Wormwood is toxic to nerve cells and in high concentrations causes seizures but the amount added as an ingredient to absinthe was far below the levels required for any effect. Nevertheless the establishment became increasingly concerned about absinthe and its popularity blaming it for degenerate behaviour (those dirty bohemians!), an increase in crime and the breakdown of society. The tabloid media of the day splashed reports of amoral deeds instigated by the nefarious influence of absinthe. Such scare stories were enough reason for successive governments to ban absinthe outright starting with the Belgian Congo in 1898, Belgium 1906, Switzerland 1910, USA 1912, and the spiritual home of *la Fée Verte*, France in 1915. Ironically Britain (where gin-thism had decimated successive generations) never outlawed it. What the authorities may have failed to consider was that it was very strong liquor with an alcohol content of between 60 and 90 per cent ABV. All the symptoms of absinthism are also those of chronic alcohol abuse so if they had legislated for a decrease in alcohol content to match that other French icon, brandy, rather than needing to outlaw it, absinthe might not have the fabled and slightly naughty reputation it has now.

Absinthe's psychoactive properties had been exaggerated by fearmongers of the early twentieth century and in the 1990s a revival of the formerly sanctioned spirit brought it back into cocktail bars and drinks cabinets.

HOW TO MAKE ABSINTHE

Ferment sugar beet or grape juice and distil the alcohol. Then take a selection of aromatic herbs and spices including the all-important wormwood. (When Pernod Fils first made their absinthe in the late eighteenth century they included aniseed, fennel, hyssop, lemon balm, angelica, star anise, dittany, juniper, nutmeg, and veronica.) Crush the botanicals and mascerate them for several days so the aromatics infuse the distilled spirit. Filter the liquor and add water then distil it again. Finally add green anise and other herbs to the distillate for colour and flavour. Here comes the Green Fairy!

La louche is the ritual of adding water to absinthe. Usually it is poured over a lump of sugar placed on a perforated spoon that rests on the top of the glass and as the water trickles through it slowly transforms the spirit from emerald green to an opalescent shade of yellow green. This opalescence is known as *la louche*. The practice of setting fire to an absinthe-soaked sugar cube and letting it burn is dramatic but not traditional – it was invented in the Czech Republic in the 1990s.

Wormwood is mentioned several times in the Bible. Both quotes below are from the King James Version.

Therefore thus saith the Lord of hosts concerning the prophets; Behold, I will feed them with wormwood, and make them drink the water of gall: for from the prophets of Jerusalem is profaneness gone forth into all the land.

(Jeremiah 23:15)

And the name of the star is called Wormwood, and the third part of the waters became wormwood; and many men died of the waters, because they were made bitter.

(Revelation 8:11)

Writers, painters and musicians venerated absinthe as their muse. Drinking it was believed to stimulate creativity. Three celebrated paintings feature the green fairy: Edouard Manet's *Absinthe Drinker*, one of the first works of the Impressionist style; Edgar Degas' *Dans un café*; and Van Gogh's *Still Life with Absinthe*. When *absintheur* and painter Henri Toulouse-Lautrec fancied a drink he would say he wanted to *'étouffer un perroquet'* (strangle a parakeet), a slang term amongst the Bohemians.

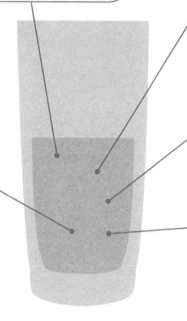

Ancient Egyptians knew *Artemisia absinthium* to be anthelmintic, meaning it had properties to expel intestinal worms – hence the name 'wormwood'. For millennia it has been used as medicine to treat a variety of ailments including rheumatism, relief for period pains and childbirth, and as a purgative – wormwood infusions were so unpalatable they caused vomiting.

Oscar Wilde was a noted absinthe drinker during the final years of his life in exile in Paris. He described one experience; 'Three nights I sat up all night drinking absinthe and thinking that I was singularly clearheaded and sane. The waiter came in and began watering the sawdust. The most wonderful flowers, tulips, lilies, and roses sprang up and made a garden in the café. "Don't you see them", I said to him. "Mais non monsieur, il n'y a rien" *(No sir, there's nothing there)'*.

Absinthe's connection with madness was well known inspiring the expression *'Un omnibus pour Charenton'* – Charenton being a lunatic asylum outside Paris. Some *absintheurs* such as Vincent Van Gogh displayed psychotic behaviour, but he was mentally ill before he started drinking absinthe. Alcohol abuse does change brain chemistry and as absinthe was so high in alcohol then heavy drinkers probably should have bought a ticket for that omnibus.

NINKASI'S NECTAR – BEER

Believe it or not beer is the third most regularly consumed drink on earth after water (number one) and tea (number two) making it by far the world's favourite alcohol. It is probably the third oldest purposely made alcoholic libation. Mead (fermented honey and water) is believed to be the earliest, followed by wine although rotting fruit that dropped off trees and started to ferment would have been the first experience of alcoholic intoxication that proto-humans had.

We have already seen that residue on pottery shards found in the Zagros mountains of Iran dated back to around 3500 BC and this is currently the oldest evidence of barley beer. But if fermented rice counts as beer, then there is proof of this on earthenware from a village called Jiahu in China that dates back to around 7000 BC. No one knows when beer was first consumed because before pottery was used for storing food and drink, wood and animal skins were employed and they rotted away leaving no archaeological record.

Historians surmise that beer was not invented, rather it was discovered – possibly by someone who ate damp baked grains that had fermented to become gently intoxicating. If that was not enough of a reason to drink beer, the nutrition it offered was second to none and it was much easier for a human body to digest those wild undomesticated cereal crops in the form of beer than it was to eat them. The first brewers most likely were women and for millennia brewing was women's work. Beer was a staple of the diet, usually made at home, and consumed by the whole family as a source of nourishment, water, and in some societies because it was part of their cultural identity. Beer was central to several

Beer is a remarkably diverse drink with over one hundred different styles such as porter, saison, IPA, dunkel, *bière de garde*, stout, or ale. As mentioned previously, pilsener lager is the most widely consumed style particularly in Africa, China and South America. Major brewing countries that developed unique styles of beer now popular around the world are (in no order of importance) Belgium, Britain, Germany, and the Czech Republic. Meanwhile, a vibrant craft-brewing scene in the USA (where brewers aren't bound by the traditions of the Old World) is having a big influence, especially in Britain. Beers with punchier hops and imaginative hybrid styles are typical of the American brewing revolution.

When the Pilgrim Fathers made landfall at Cape Cod in 1620 on their way to the New World it was not their intended destination. The plan was to sail further south but on the three-month journey from England they ran low on supplies, especially one crucial commodity leading William Bradford, one of the group's leaders, to note in his journal: 'We could not now take time for further search or consideration, our victuals being much spent, especially our beere.'

The yard-of-ale trick where beer is consumed in one go from a long glass tube stems from cultures such as the Vikings who used hollow animal horns as drinking vessels. Horns were pointed so could not be placed on a flat surface. If the drinker wanted to rest his or her arms they would have to drain the contents before putting down the horn.

Several myths abound on the provenance of India Pale Ale (IPA) – usually along the lines that it was highly hopped ale made specifically for the Indian market and brewed extra strong to last the journey where it was destined for eighteenth-century soldiers guarding Britain's interests. According to beer historians this is the story. A brewer named George Hodgson based in the East End of London (near to the docks where ships trading with the Indies moored) was already making a strong pale hopped beer brewed in October for keeping over winter. It was referred to in a 1768 pamphlet as 'October malt wine'. Ship captains looking for goods to sell in India including beer bought Hodgson's brews and the October ale in particular became highly popular with customers. During the four-month voyage from London the beer matured much quicker than it would have done in Blighty and so arrived at its destination in peak condition. By luck George Hodgson was already brewing the perfect beer for export to India and he was in the right place at the right time to capitalise on it, building a lucrative trade. Other brewers started to brew their own versions of October ale and undercut Hodgson's prices to grab a share of the market, not least Bass in Burton-upon-Trent. Around 1829 the beer became known as East India Pale Ale and a domestic version also became popular with Britain's beer drinkers eventually evolving into that most iconic of British beers – 'a pint of bitter'.

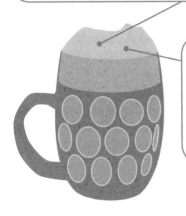

Would I were in an alehouse in London! I would give all my fame for a pot of ale, and safety.

William Shakespeare, *Henry V* (Act III, scene ii)

ancient civilisations who believed it was a gift from the gods. It has always had magical abilities to spread joy, conviviality, and build bonds between people.

Early beer did not contain hops so honey, herbs, spices, and plants such as wormwood, henbane, dandelion, mint, and bog myrtle were added for flavour.

The earliest written evidence of hops being used in brewing beer comes from the French Benedictine monastery of Corbie, near Amiens, in AD 822. Beer containing hops was first documented in England around 1361 when it was imported into Great Yarmouth from Amsterdam. Residents of the British Isles consumed ale – a malty sweet liquor that contained no hops. But the continental Europeans with their hopped beverage called beer had a secret weapon – as well as hops imparting bitterness and aroma, they are also a natural preservative so beer lasted for weeks without going sour unlike ale which went off quickly. For decades after hops were introduced to Britain ale *and* beer were consumed but eventually brewers stopped brewing unhopped ale and concentrated on beer as it was more profitable and had a longer life. Nowadays almost all commercially brewed beer worldwide contains hops and the words 'beer' and 'ale' are interchangeable terms that mean the same thing.

Knowledge of beer travelled around the world through trade, conquest, and reputation although isolated societies such as Amazon Indians also drank beer – made from corn – so it appears that fermented cereal beverages developed independently in different areas over the millennia. Romans considered beer to be *déclassé* and instead they revered wine. Beer was something that their hairy barbarian enemies in northern Europe drank to excess. Saxons were bingeing beer drinkers as were other Germanic tribes. When the former landed in England in the fifth century they found natives were already very enthusiastic consumers of strong ale that led to a familiar state known in Old English as *beordruncen* or 'very drunk'.

For thousands of years beer was a staple that everyone, children included, consumed prodigiously for breakfast, with their main meal, before bed and at times in between. Not only did it provide valuable nutrition but it meant people did not have to risk drinking polluted water. Beer consumed as an alternative to water was known in English as 'small beer' due to its low alcohol content. That term is still used today to denote something worthless, although to our ancestors it was anything but as it undoubtedly saved them from contracting waterborne diseases.

Britain's increasing influence overseas and vast trading network spread the demand for beer and introduced it to parts of the world where it had not previously been. Ships carried beer as a source of drinking water, and for daily rations to keep the sailors content. Colonists settling in countries such as America, Australia and New Zealand exported their desire for beer. As Britain's empire grew it made sense to build breweries in the colonies rather than rely on imported beer – consequently the sun never set on the brewing of the world's most popular alcoholic drink. That has been the case ever since as every few seconds somewhere on earth a person cracks open a bottle of the nectar of the gods.

William Shakespeare's father was an ale-conner in Stratford in 1557. This sought-after official position entailed testing beer quality in a local jurisdiction and checking that customers were not being overcharged. Also known as *gustator cervisiae* it was an important job in an era when ale was such a staple. Ale-conners had the authority to send anyone serving poor-quality beer or fleecing patrons to the manor court. There is no contemporary evidence for the widely reported lore that ale-conners wore leather britches and would pour ale onto a bench and then sit in it for half an hour. If when they stood up the britches stuck to the bench the beer was supposedly poor quality. This myth is perpetuated by the City of London Ale-Connors who wear leather britches and sit in a pool of beer when they go out ale testing. Nowadays the rank exists solely for ceremonial reasons and fun.

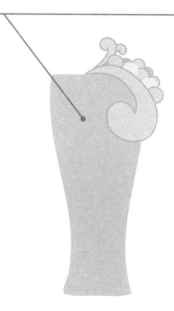

HOW BEER IS MADE

Brewing beer is a form of alchemy. Wort – sugary water from malted barley (sometimes with added wheat, oats, rice, rye or corn) – and hops are boiled together and then cooled. Some brewers will add cultured yeast to the brew while others open the window and wait for whatever yeast spores are floating in the air to land. The yeast voraciously consumes sugar in the brew and converts it to alcohol and carbon dioxide by the process of fermentation. As if by magic it turns into beer. That sounds very simple and in theory it is. Most people could probably make beer but whether it would be drinkable is another matter. Brewing is an art and a science. Balancing the flavours to perfection takes skill and creating the optimum conditions to make the yeast happy is essential.

On the family tree of beer there are three branches – ale, lager, and lambic. All three are made by combining water, cereal, hops and yeast. With ales the brewer adds a species of yeast called *Saccharomyces cerevisiae* which in addition to creating alcohol and carbon dioxide through a quick fermentation also contributes fruity aromas and flavours to the beer. Lager brewers add *Saccharomyces pastorianus* yeast. This slowly ferments the sugars in the brew and converts them to alcohol and carbon dioxide to give the beer a crisp body, but it contributes little in aroma or flavour. Ale and lager are made with the brewer's pet cultured yeasts, whereas lambic beers (traditionally made in Payottenland south west of Brussels) rely on spontaneous fermentation by a variety of wild yeasts, often *Brettanomyces,* and other microflora that live in the brewery building and in the local atmosphere. *Terroir* at its most distinctive. This style of fermentation and lengthy maturation imparts a tangy sourness to lambic beers which some people think

Many women profess not to like beer because they find it bitter. Women have a lower tolerance to bitterness than men do and conversely men are more sensitive to sweetness. Bitterness in nature is often a signal of something harmful and so humans have evolved to be wary of it. We are one thousand times more sensitive to bitter compounds than sweet. In Palaeolithic times, men were the hunters but women were the gatherers of berries, fruit, and grains, and tasted and tested as they went along. Anything bitter they would most likely avoid in case it was toxic. Luckily that did not apply to beer though because early brews would have been sweet.

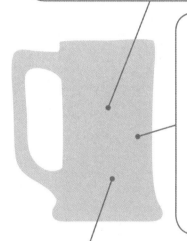

The epitome of beer worship occurs in the Thai Buddhist temple colloquially known as *Wat Lan Khuat* or 'the Temple of a Million Bottles'. Walls and roofs of the complex of over twenty buildings including temple, prayer rooms, and bedrooms are constructed with around 1.5 million empty green Heineken and brown Chang beer bottles. According to the monks the bottles provide good lighting, are easy to clean, and do not lose their colour. Even the beer caps are used – to make mosaics of the Buddha.

The *Reinheitsgebot* or Purity Law was initiated in Bavaria in 1516 and restricted the permitted ingredients of beer to water, barley, and hops. Yeast was not included because no one knew at the time the crucial role that it played. When German Unification was ratified in 1871 the Bavarians insisted that their protectionist regulation became national law much to the chagrin of brewers who included rye, spices, and fruit in the beer. European Union law demanded the *Reinheitsgebot* be abolished so now German brewers have more freedom although many choose out of tradition to adhere to the old law.

taste more like wine, cider or sherry than beer. After fermentation the brewer has options of what to do with the beer – sell it as cask-conditioned ale, kegged beer, bottle-conditioned beer, or bottled pasteurised beer.

Cask-conditioned ale, also known as real ale, is the style of beer that most traditional British pubs serve. This is beer at its most natural – unfiltered and unpasteurised. Due to the presence of living yeast in the cask a secondary fermentation takes place adding even more flavour and condition. When the suspended yeast cells have dropped to the bottom of the cask the beer is ready to drink. It is dispensed into the glass via a hand pump which pulls it through a pipe from the cellar. Very strong beers can be kept in a cask for months where they will continue to mature, but with lower alcohol everyday 'session' beers once the cask is opened to the air it needs to be consumed quickly because after three to four days it starts to go stale. By around seven days it may have turned sour. If that happens mention the vinegary taste to the bar staff and they should replace the offending drink. Free beer! If the cask has not been opened, the beer should last around five weeks in good condition.

Kegged beer is filtered, pasteurised by quickly heating it, carbonated with carbon dioxide (and sometimes an injection of nitrogen), and packaged in a pressurised container. It is dispensed by opening a tap on the bar; the pressure within the keg forces it through the pipe. Unlike cask-conditioned ale this beer no longer contains living yeast cells so the shelf life is much longer. Low- to medium-strength kegged beers normally last for up to six weeks once the keg is opened, and up to six months unopened.

Bottled beer comes in two versions – pasteurised and filtered as with the kegged beer; or bottle conditioned. The latter is the nearest thing to cask-conditioned ale and depending on the brewer some of beer destined for the cask is bottled and sealed; or the beer is filtered and then reseeded with yeast so a secondary fermentation takes place in the bottle and creates carbon dioxide so the beer tingles on the tongue. After a few weeks the yeast goes dormant and drops to the bottom as a sediment. A high alcohol beer with yeast in the bottle will age over the years and change its character. To investigate how beer can change over time, buy a case of twelve bottle-conditioned beers above 8 per cent ABV and try one each year, making notes on how the beer has changed. It may start to resemble rich fruit cake. If Christmas cake in a bottle does not appeal, then send it to me…

SERVING TEMPERATURE

This depends where in the world the beer is being served. Australia and the USA in particular prefer carbonated beer cold enough to cause frostbite. In Britain (the land of warm flat beer as the Aussies say), the ideal temperature for ale is 12 °C and for lagers 3–8 °C. Temperature is especially important because if beer is too cold, the flavours will be muted. Although with certain beers some might say that is a good idea.

BURNT WINE – BRANDY

Brandy, as anyone who has ever had the lining of their throat melted by that particular fire water will not be surprised to learn, derives its name from the English translation of a Dutch word *brandewijn* meaning 'burnt wine'.

Arab alchemists in the eighth century had experimented with distillation of fruits and flowers to make perfume and medicinal spirit *eau de vie*. As Arab influence expanded into Spain, Portugal and southern France with the Moorish occupation, so knowledge of distilling moved into wine-producing areas such as Cognac. Medieval Dutch traders who bought wine from the western coastal region of France introduced distilled wine to northern Europe. Brandy is concentrated wine so the Dutch intended to dilute it on arrival. But the spirit improved during transportation through contact with the oak barrels it was stored in, mellowing its intensity and adding aroma, flavour and colour. This new drink was far too good to dilute and *brandewijn* entered the lexicon and the drinks cabinets of the discerning tippler.

Brandy was not just something to drink; it was a handy preservative, antiseptic, and painkiller so it became an invaluable commodity on ships. By the mid-seventeenth century the Netherlands was the world's greatest maritime trading nation so the reputation of *brandewijn* spread far. In the eighteenth century African slavers began to

Admiral Horatio (Lord) Nelson's body was preserved in brandy after his death at the Battle of Trafalgar so it could be returned to England. To prevent the corpse from decomposing during its transportation from Trafalgar to Gibraltar it was stored in a leaguer – a large oak water barrel filled with brandy, surgical spirit and camphor. Rumo᠆ that sailors tapped the cask and dr᠆ brandy are fanciful – the leaguer wa᠆ to a mast under a permanent guard.᠆ arrived on the 'Rock' the leaguer was᠆ with spirit for the six-week journey ᠆ *Victory* back to London for a state f᠆ perfectly pickled.

Until the mid-nineteenth century in some Western c᠆ a practice called heroic medicine cures was comm᠆ treatment for certain ailments. This entailed patients ᠆ great amounts of alcohol. Prince Albert, husband of ᠆ Victoria was prescribed six pints of brandy a day to cure᠆ typhoid. He died.

Britain is an island so smuggling is impossible to prevent. For centuries there were few periods when the nation was not at war with France. In those times brandy imports were either banned or heavily taxed as a way of punishing the enemy across the Channel. Smuggling became a lucrative trade especially in Essex, Kent, Sussex, Devon, and Cornwall. It is estimated that in the years between 1780 and 1783 when the population of Britain was only around 7.5 million, 13 million gallons of brandy were smuggled into the country. It was not just the Del Boys who were up to it – even pillars of the community had a hand in it or turned a blind eye. Some vicars stored contraband in church crypts, local squires expected a cut of the brandy booty, and excisemen could be bought off. As Rudyard Kipling wrote in his poem 'A Smugglers' Song':

Five and twenty ponies,
Trotting through the dark –
Brandy for the Parson,
'Baccy for the Clerk;
Them that asks no questions isn't told a lie –
Watch the wall, my darling, while the Gentlemen go by!

Smugglers landed the goods on shore then inland gangs took over to hide, distribute and sell them. An intricate network of tunnels and storage chambers was set up so loot could be transferred inland and hidden, often in the cellars of pubs, hence the reason why The Smugglers' Inn is a fairly common name.

St Bernard hounds, those enormous beasts with the mournful eyes that work as mountain rescue dogs are indelibly associated with brandy hung in a tiny cask from their collars. The story goes that when people caught in a blizzard are discovered by the dog they can warm up with a tot of brandy. But according to the monks of St Bernard's Hospice in the Swiss Alps the story is not true – none of their dogs has ever carried brandy. It seems that the legend is Victorian whimsy inspired by the paintings of English artists John Emms and Edwin Landseer, both of whom portrayed St Bernard dogs with casks around their necks.

Syllabub is now a dense creamy fruit pudding but it was originally a spicy mulled milk drink flavoured with brandy, rum or port. When spirits were not available cider would suffice and the milk was already warm when it was sourced directly from the cow. A similar drink known as caudle was popular during the Middle Ages as a soothing potation for the sick and contained bread, eggs, sugar and spices. The name derives from Old French *caudel* which itself came from the Latin word for warm – *calidus*.

Brandy is best served in a brandy snifter or balloon because the wide base of the glass narrows towards the top concentrating the aromas. When tasting it do not swirl the liquid around in the glass because volatile flavours can be lost.

Moonraker is the nickname of people from Wiltshire. Legend tells of a gang of smugglers who had concealed casks of brandy in a pond and were caught one moonlit night by customs officers trying to retrieve their goods with the help of a rake. The smugglers explained that there was a large cheese in the pond but they were having trouble pulling it towards the bank. The excisemen left them to it, and went off laughing at the stupid country folk who didn't know it was the moon's reflection.

accept brandy as currency and it soon became such a mark of distinction that slavers preferred it over guns and baubles. Some would accept nothing else as payment for the human cargo they were selling for export to the New World. When in the 1650s the Dutch East Indies trading company set up a settlement on the Cape of Good Hope to resupply ships going to and from Europe and the Indies, one of the first actions was to plant vines and as soon as wine was produced in the Cape Colony, distilling followed with a harsh spirit nicknamed *witblits*, or white lightning.

Brandy not made with grapes must be labelled 'fruit brandy'. Calvados from Normandy is distilled apple juice, as is applejack in the USA. Grappa, the Italian brandy, is made by distilling the grape pulp, skins and stems left over after most of the juice has been extracted to make wine. Schnapps is the name for fruit brandy produced in Germany or Austria. In Balkans countries such as Croatia, Macedonia, and Montenegro it is known as rakia and made from pears, cherries, plums, or apricots. Each bottle of rakia should be sold with the phone number of the local fire brigade such is its heat.

Brandy from the Cognac and Armagnac regions remains the benchmark by which all other brandies are measured; both those names are protected by a geographical designation. Unless the grapes are grown in those regions and the juice distilled there it cannot legally be called cognac or armagnac. Until it was usurped by Scotch whisky as the luxury spirit in China in the early years of the twenty-first century, cognac was *ne plus ultra* when it came to showing off. Offering guests a glass of premium brandy was a way of displaying wealth. The amber colour of the drink was all important – it meant the spirit had been aged for years in wood and could not be mistaken for cheap clear spirit such as ropey old vodka. Sales of cognac in the USA shot up in the 1990s when rap singers started showing off their wealth and good taste by buying the most expensive labels following a centuries-old tradition of brandy being more than a bottle of burnt wine.

HOW TO MAKE BRANDY

Wine is heated in a still until the alcohol condenses. Chemical reactions happen during distillation that add aroma to the spirit. The concentrated distillate is run off into oak barrels, or may be blended with other brandies and then it is left to age for a few years. In that time the spirit will gain colour and flavour compounds from the wood and the longer it ages the more complex and smooth it will be.

A French brandy label uses shorthand to describe its quality and age. These are the most common:

A.C. – aged two years in wood

V.S. – 'Very Special' three star; means aged in wood for at least three years

V.S.O.P. – 'Very Superior Old Pale' five star; means aged in wood for at least five years

X.O. – 'Extra Old' aged in wood for at least six years

Snap-dragon was a popular British parlour game played in winter, especially at Christmas. To play it place raisins in a shallow bowl, pour brandy over them and light the spirit. Pluck the raisins out of the flames and eat them. The eighteenth-century polymath Dr Samuel Johnson described it in his *Dictionary of the English Language* (1755) as 'a play in which they catch raisins out of burning brandy and, extinguishing them by closing the mouth, eat them'.

In Britain, a land that never turned down the chance of a drink, brandy was embraced like a lost child leading to rhapsodic quotes such as this by Samuel Johnson: 'Claret is the liquor for boys; port for men; but he who aspires to be a hero must drink brandy'.

APPLES AND PEARS –
CIDER AND PERRY

What have the Kazakhstanis ever done for us? Shared with us the fruit of *Malus sieversii* for one thing. Better known as the wild apple, it is the ancestor of the domesticated apple. Where would teachers and fruit bowls be without it? More importantly what would cider drinkers do?

Britons are the world's biggest producers and consumers of cider and 45 per cent of apples grown in Blighty are used to make it. There is also a tradition of cider in Ireland, France (Normandy and Brittany), Spain (Basque region, Galicia and Asturias), Germany, Argentina, the USA, Australia, and Sweden.

When the Romans invaded England in AD 43 they found the indigenous Celts revered the apple and were partial to cider – possibly mixed with honey and water. The Romans did a great favour by organising and classifying apples and introducing new varieties. But it was another group of invaders, the Normans from 1066, who gave cider a boost and enhanced the orchards by bringing new cultivars. By the beginning of the fourteenth century, cider was being made in almost every county in England, even as far north as Yorkshire.

Some people believe the English were conquered by the French because the Normans came across the water from France. But Norman means 'North Man'; in other words the cuckoos in the Normandy nest were Vikings who had moved south from Scandinavia in the early ninth century. Vikings were keen cider drinkers and this explains why in France, a land dominated by wine, there is a proud tradition of cider in Normandy.

Even now when Britain is a largely urban society, cider is seen (often with misty eyes) as a bucolic potation drunk by jolly country folk at village fêtes – a Thomas Hardy idyll. Cider was traditionally a rural drink because until the Industrial Revolution Britain was fundamentally a rural society. Most farms had a few apple trees and in some areas until the end of the nineteenth century farm labourers received part of their wage in cider. Soil conditions and climate in the West Country of Somerset, Herefordshire, and Worcestershire ideally suited apple cultivation and even today most cider is produced in those areas by the world's largest cider makers including HP Bulmer.

Of the 7,500+ apple varietals, hundreds are used for cider making rather than eating. Cider apples are divided into four categories according to their flavour: *sweets* – low in acidity and tannins; *bitter sweets* – low in acidity, high in tannins; *sharps* – high in acidity, low in tannins; and *bitter sharps* – high in acidity and tannins. Cider apples have higher tannin concentrations than their eating counterparts. Tannins are substances that enhance flavour, give cider its 'bite', add body, and help to preserve it. In high levels they can be very astringent. Without a decent amount of tannin cider would be insipid which is why eating apples are not ideal unless they are blended with cider apples.

Cider entered the English language in a circuitous route from the French *cidre*, which derived from the Latin *sicera*. This was a version of the Greek *sikera* which itself originally came from the Hebrew *shekar* meaning 'any intoxicating drink other than wine made by the fermentation of fruit juice'.

When British Prime Minister John Stuart, third Earl of Bute, decided in 1763 that the Exchequer needed refilling after the coffers-draining Seven Years' War, he turned his gaze to cider and increased taxes on it. What he failed to consider was that cider was the drink of the common person and they were not happy to pay more for it. Effigies of Bute were hung on trees and burnt in the streets, while the pamphlets and newspapers lampooned him. It was not long before he was forced to resign and the tax was repealed in 1766.

Between the fourteenth century and the nineteenth century, Western Europe underwent a period of cooling known as the Little Ice Age. In England vineyards suffered and wine production decreased. Apples survived in cooler temperatures and so began a golden age for cider. Two other factors came into play – both political. First, the wars with France and Spain interrupted wine, brandy, and sherry imports; and, second, the execution of King Charles I in 1649 and the subsequent republic under Oliver Cromwell had the effect of making aristocratic courtiers redundant. They retired to their country estates and some of them started experimenting with cider, cross-pollination of apple cultivars, glassware, and corks. The fact that seventeenth-century cider makers were producing sparkling cider by a secondary fermentation in a bottle made from reinforced glass and sealed with a cork is incontrovertible as the written proof is in papers stored

in the archive of the Royal Society in London. The significance of this is that they were doing it before the man widely credited as inventing champagne, Dom Pérignon, was born. In other words, West Country cider makers were the real progenitors of one of France's greatest sources of national pride. This subject is covered in more detail in the chapter about sparkling wine.

During the Napoleonic Wars (1792–1815) farmers in counties such as Herefordshire were pressured into producing grain and livestock to ensure a domestic supply, so cider orchards were neglected. As nineteenth-century commercial producers increased in size, small farmers started selling off apple-growing land to those powerful businesses. Ancient orchards were destroyed and with them old cider apple cultivars. By the 1960s big producers were growing fewer tannin-rich intensely flavoursome varieties of apple in order to make bland and easy-drinking cider. This also coincided

with the growth of pasteurised beer which in some people's opinion turned a beautiful natural brew into a fizzy standardised product with no personality. By the 1980s cider was in trouble. It was perceived as being uncool, a drink for rustic men who resembled scarecrows, or as cheap loony juice that teenagers necked in bus shelters. An unexpected saviour appeared on the scene in the early twenty-first century in the guise of an Irish brand called Magners. When the Irish company C&C Group launched their bottled cider in the UK with a series of slick TV adverts of young gorgeous professional men and women drinking cider outside in warm and beautiful countryside they really grabbed attention. In pubs and bars the staff were instructed to serve Magners over ice. This was genius because a pint glass filled with ice cubes would not have the space to fit in all the cider from the bottle so customers had to take it with them to their seat where others would notice the brand. Suddenly Magners was ubiquitous and its most enthusiastic supporters were men and women in their twenties – a new generation of cider drinkers. This unwitting revolution has saved farmhouse cider in Britain by creating a vast interest in the craft producers of that ancient drink. Cider is in a second golden age. Long may it last – wæs hæl!

Old Twelfth Night (17 January) is wassail season, when keen cider drinkers gather in orchards, traditionally in Devon, Herefordshire, and Somerset. One tree known as Apple Tree Man is chosen as the focus of the ceremony. Pieces of bread soaked in cider are hung from the boughs to attract good spirits and cider is poured onto the roots. To arouse the orchard from hibernation, the wassailers make a hullabaloo by beating pots and pans; then gunshots are fired through the crown of Apple Tree Man to scare off evil forces. Finally a toast is downed and everyone shouts out 'wæs hæl' (Old English for 'good health') and sings a ditty along the lines of:

Wassail, wassail all round the town
The zider-cup's white and the zider's brown
Our zider is made vrom good apple trees.

Scottish cider producer Thistly Cross were looking for a unique selling point and borrowed some whisky barrels from Glenglassaugh distillery in which to mature cider. After the cider had been bottled, Glenglassaugh were intrigued by what the cider might have added to the wood, and they took back the barrels to fill with whisky. At the time of writing, the world's first whisky to be aged in a cider cask is quietly maturing in a warehouse in Aberdeenshire.

What is scrumpy? Opinions vary and there is no legal definition. To some people it is the most rustic and authentic cider – a no-nonsense strong, flat and murky concoction made from real apples rather than concentrate. To others it is any cider made with apples from a variety of sources – windfall, begged, borrowed, or 'scrumped' i.e. nicked from a tree.

An apple a day keeps the doctor away especially if it is in the form of cider, or so people in the seventeenth century thought. To 'smele to an old swete apple' was believed to build a person's strength after illness. Cider vinegar was an ancient remedy for weight loss and widely used as an antiseptic. Diarist and arborist John Evelyn wrote: 'Generally all strong and pleasant cider excites and cleanses the stomach, strengthens digestion, and infallibly frees the kidneys and bladder from breeding the gravel stone'. Cider's laxative effect was thought to cure melancholy by purging black bile in a process called 'dissolving the belly'. A remedy for scarlet fever involved sweating it out with the help of a pint of mulled spiced cider. Cider was carried on seventeenth- and eighteenth-century ships as a remedy for scurvy which was a scourge on long voyages. Those ship captains, including Captain Cook, were right – in 1948 Britain's Medical Research Council carried out experiments on cider and reported that a daily glass of scrumpy could prevent scurvy.

If you travel to the USA beware if someone offers you a cider. It will be harmless spiced apple juice. The real thing is known as 'hard cider'.

PERRY

Apples and pears. Cider and perry. That often misunderstood drink called perry was most likely introduced to England after the Norman Conquest and *poiré* is still popular in Normandy.

Perry is *not* pear cider – that is a sweet commercially produced fizzy beverage from concentrated pear juice with large amounts of added sugar. Perry is made from pears with such high levels of astringent tannins that anyone eating them would feel as though their face had turned inside out. Some of the sugars in perry pears do not ferment so perry has a residual sweetness with the dry peppery character of the tannins hiding underneath.

Perry pears have high levels of an unfermentable sugar called sorbitol. An unexpected side effect of this sugar is its laxative properties, hence the reputation perry has for going 'down like velvet, round like thunder, and out like lightning'.

Question: What was the first alcoholic drink to be advertised on British TV and why was it revolutionary? Answer: Babycham in 1957 and it was directed at women. No alcohol before had been specifically targeted at females. Anyone who has tasted Babycham might believe it is just pop because it is so light, but as the advertising said at the time, it was 'genuine champagne perry'. Babycham was invented in 1953 by Shepton Mallet brewer Francis Showering and immediately became a favourite, especially with Great-Aunt Sabina and Grandma Margaret. Latterly its popularity has waned but it is still produced in its original Somerset hometown where a giant plastic model of a cartoon fawn, the brand's immediately recognisable mascot, is a local landmark.

There is poetry in the names of cider apple and perry pear varieties. Who could resist drinking a cider made with one or more of these beauties: Handsome Norman, Irish Peach, Foxwhelp, Brown Snout, Improved Dove, Watson's Dumpling, Brabant Bellefleur, Slack ma Girdle, or Golden Knob?

Blakeney Red is the most widely cultivated perry pear but producers have hundreds of varieties to choose from with some especially evocative names including: Snake Pole, Tumper, Swan Egg, Merrylegs, Early Treacle, Bastard Longdon, and Golden Balls.

Traditionally the heartland of perry production in England was the same region as cider making, with the inclusion of Monmouthshire in Wales. Perry's popularity was at a zenith when cider was in its first golden age in the seventeenth and eighteenth centuries. Perry pear trees are challenging, however – they can take up to 100 years to mature, and are labour intensive to harvest. As tastes and agricultural practices changed in the mid-twentieth century around the same time cider started to decline, perry manufacturers turned to varieties of pears that could also be eaten, so the final product was wishy-washy without enough of those all-important tannins to give it a kick. Where cider's saviour was Magners, so perry received life support from Brothers pear cider. This fruity drink made from concentrated pear juice started to appear on the bar at music festivals in the mid-1990s. Those Brothers know a thing or two about pears as they are members of the Showering family, inventors of Babycham, the original sparkling perry. Word spread about pear cider and this led inquisitive drinkers to investigate real perry. Just like the farmhouse cider makers who are flourishing thanks to the resurgence in cider drinking, perry is once again on the menu.

For centuries it was common for English farm labourers to receive part of their wages in cider – up to six pints a day, and thrice that amount at harvest time. This was not high-quality cider; it was diluted 'small cider' which had nicknames such as ciderkin, and pomepirken. Labourers carried their cider around in small wooden casks called castrells. Cider was also currency and could be used for payment of rent and church tithes. In 1887 the government added a clause to the Truck Act in an attempt to prohibit payment of wages in cider rather than the coin of the realm. (An earlier Truck Act of 1831 hadn't stopped the practice as it didn't apply to agricultural workers.) No more liquid pay packets.

If the fruit of the tree of knowledge was an apple does that mean that Adam and Eve could have brewed cider? After all the Garden of Eden was located somewhere in the Middle East which is the area where wine and beer was first made in antiquity. Perhaps not because there is a theory that the apple in Eden was actually a pomegranate. Perhaps someone made a mistake when translating the Bible because the name pomegranate derives from the Latin for 'seeded apple' – *Pomum granatum*.

HOW CIDER IS MADE

Real cider is fermented single varietal or blended apple juice with nothing added, and nothing taken away. Apples in the orchard are harvested, washed, sorted, and scratted (pulped) into pomace. The pomace is transferred to a cider press until all the 'must' or juice is squeezed out and drained into vats or oak casks. Wild yeast that lives in the apple skins, oak casks, or in the atmosphere around the farm ferments the sugars for several weeks. After that it is transferred into different oak casks, sealed and left to age for up to three years. Then the flat and cloudy cider is ready to drink, or it might be filtered and pasteurised to give it a longer life, carbonated and then bottled.

Major commercial producers normally make cider from blended apple concentrate (including imported) that is treated with sulphur dioxide to inhibit wild yeasts. Cultured yeast is used for predictable behaviour during fermentation, with ammonium sulphate to speed up the process. Artificial colourings, sweeteners and preservatives are added before the cider is filtered, pasteurised and carbonated.

Traditional perry is made in almost the same way as real cider except that the perry pomace is left to stand for some time in order to smoothen the tannins.

BUTTRESSED BOOZE – FORTIFIED WINE

Poor sherry, that much maligned and misunderstood wine many people think is only worth slugging into trifle. Port does not fare much better either when it is drowned in lemonade. What did sherry and port do to deserve such disrespect, becoming relegated to what great aunts drink at weddings? Maybe it is the sweet and cloying nature of some sherry and port and the fact that it is served in elegant small glasses that dowagers sit and nurse. There is a reason for the diminutive size. Port and sherry are strong in alcohol – that's why they are called 'fortified' wine. Fortification comes from adding distilled grape spirit – often brandy – so the wine ends up with a kick at between 15 per cent and 22 per cent ABV.

PORT

Vinho do Porto, better known in English as port originated in Portugal's Douro Valley. Politics influenced the development of the industry when England was at war with France (when weren't they?). Portugal, England's oldest ally, was a reliable source of wine when French wine was hard to procure, punitively taxed or banned in Britain. Bordeaux had to be sacrificed for the sake of Blighty. Beneficial trade privileges between Britain and Portugal sealed by the Methuen Treaty of 1703 meant that Portuguese *vinho* was subject to lower import taxes than French *vin*. Port became known as the English gentleman's drink and the influence of British involvement in the burgeoning eighteenth-century port trade is still apparent in the names of two of the best known brands – Croft and Sandeman.

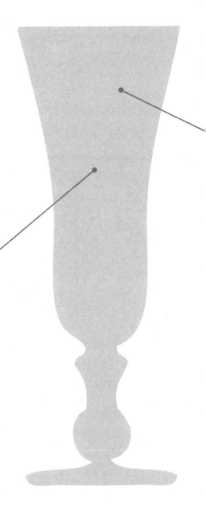

The Poet Laureate of Great Britain is an honorary position where the holder is generally expected to compose poems to mark important national occasions. In addition to an annual stipend, the Poet Laureate is also entitled to a 'butt of sack' – translation, a huge barrel of sherry equivalent to approximately 600 bottles. This vinous reward dates from the Restoration era (1660) when sack was the most fashionable drink.

William Shakespeare must have been quite taken with sherry to write such a rhapsodic speech for Sir John Falstaff, avaricious erstwhile companion to Prince Hal in the play *Henry IV Part 2*. This is an excerpt:

A good sherris sack hath a two-fold operation in it. It ascends me into the brain; dries me there all the foolish and dull and curdy vapours which environ it; makes it apprehensive, quick, forgetive, full of nimble fiery and delectable shapes, which, delivered o'er to the voice, the tongue, which is the birth, becomes excellent wit. The second property of your excellent sherris is, the warming of the blood; which, before cold and settled, left the liver white and pale, which is the badge of pusillanimity and cowardice; but the sherris warms it and makes it course from the inwards to the parts extreme: it illumineth the face, which as a beacon gives warning to all the rest of this little kingdom, man, to arm; and then the vital commoners and inland petty spirits muster me all to their captain, the heart, who, great and puffed up with this retinue, doth any deed of courage; and this valour comes of sherries.

SHERRY

Sherry is an anglicised pronunciation of the town of Jerez in Andalusia which was called *Šeriš* (pronounced 'sherish') by the Arab-speaking Moors who occupied southern Spain from AD 711. The region's largest city Cádiz was founded in the tenth century BC by Phoenician traders who were renowned for viticulture. Successive occupiers – the ancient Greeks, Carthaginians and Romans also had winemaking expertise. Wine from this area was highly regarded and widely traded. When the region came under the rule of the Moors from North Africa starting in AD 711 they introduced the skills of distilling, albeit for medicine and perfume making, not moonshine. Local wine producers experimented by adding distilled grape spirit to the local *vino* and sherry was born – although its birth date is unknown.

During the age of exploration beginning in the late fifteenth century, several voyages started from Cádiz including journeys by Christopher Columbus and Ferdinand Magellan to the New World. Both explorers carried ample supplies of sherry and other wines aboard the fleets – it was a necessity to keep sailors happy and also as an alternative to unsafe drinking water. On one of Magellan's voyages more money was spent on wine than on armaments.

By the early sixteenth century, sherry was becoming very fashionable in England. Sherris as it was known had the benefit of no export tax levied on it and English merchants had preferential trading status in one of the region's wine exporting ports, Sanlúcar. All was sunny between England and Spain until King Henry VIII decided to pension off his Spanish wife Catherine of Aragon and divorce her in favour of Anne Boleyn. This led to schism between England, the Church of Rome and Catholic Spain culminating in the Spanish Armada and its intended invasion of Albion. Admiral

Sir Francis Drake managed to delay the launch of the Armada by a year when in 1587 his fleet sailed into Cádiz shipyard and burned the Spanish ships. Drake referred to his raid as 'singeing the beard of the King of Spain'. He also 'rescued' a consignment of 2,900 butts of sherry intended for export to South America. A butt contains approximately 600 bottles so the equivalent of around 1,740,000 ended up in a Tudor England thirsty to consume the spoils of war.

Conflict in Europe with the War of the Spanish Succession in the eighteenth century and later the Napoleonic Wars affected the fortunes of sherry producers by limiting access to formerly lucrative markets. Although in the short term this was punitive, in the long term it had a positive effect because reduced sales meant the wine was left in barrels and as it oxidised, the wine developed nutty flavours that eventually became a hallmark of sherry and were sought after by customers. As new wine was produced, winemakers would use it to top up the barrels that older wine was ageing in. As the young wine blended with the old it had a dramatic effect on aroma and flavour. This was the start of the *solera* system for ageing sherry – still in use today and which gives the wine such a distinctive character.

MADEIRA

Madeira wine comes from the eponymous Portuguese islands off the Atlantic coast of Africa. The islands' geographic position made them a handy provisioning point for European ships travelling to the Indies and the New World. By the fifteenth century there was a dynamic trade of locally produced wine even though the terrain and climate is not ideal for viticulture. It was the strategic location on shipping routes that prompted entrepreneurs to establish

In the ten most significant toasts in history this one is surely near the top. America's founding fathers sitting in a Philadelphia tavern in 1776 raised a glass of Madeira to seal their revolutionary intent as they signed the Declaration of Independence. Madeira was enormously popular in America so when the British rulers back in London levied increased duties on its import into New England this greatly disgruntled the locals. One of the signatories of the declaration, John Hancock was amongst the wealthiest merchants in the colony, not least because of his lucrative trade in importing wine – legal and illegal. In 1768 one of his ships, the *Liberty*, carrying a smuggled cargo of more than 3,000 gallons of Madeira was impounded in Boston harbour by British customs officials. Bostonians rioted and during the melee the booty was liberated and the officials run out of town. Such dissent could not be tolerated and the British government sent a gunboat to ensure it did not happen again. This fuelled the growing resentment amongst New Englanders to their masters in Britain and was one more step on the road to revolution.

Sack is an antiquated English word dating from the early fifteenth century to describe sherry, and wine from Madeira and the Canary Islands. There are several theories about the origin of the name: that it is related to the Latin word for 'dry' *siccus*; or a town called Xique. It is more likely to be from the Spanish verb *sacar* (to draw out). Notes from a meeting of the Jerez town council in 1435 refer to export wines as *sacas*.

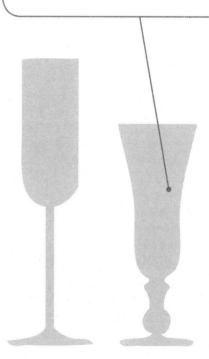

a wine-making industry to capitalise on the trade from passing vessels. Initially the wine was not fortified and would have spoiled during weeks at sea but with the addition of grape spirit or distilled cane sugar, Madeira came to resemble what we drink today.

There are four major styles of Madeira named for the grapes used to make it:

Sercial – very dry and acidic

Verdelho – medium dry with high acidity

Bual – medium sweet and rich with dried fruit flavours

Malvasia (also known as malmsey) – sweet, rich and full bodied with caramel flavours

HOW TO MAKE PORT

Ferment red or white grape juice as though making regular wine but arrest the fermentation by adding grape spirit, *aguardente*. As the fermentation is not completed it leaves residual sugars which account for port's sweet taste. Most commonly consumed as a dessert wine or *digestif* it comes in sweet, dry, tawny red and white varieties. Depending on the quality or style of port it will be matured in a specific way.

Ruby port is the most widely produced style and it is meant to be drunk 'young'. Ruby ports are blends of wine usually aged for a year in wood and then matured for two years in a bottle before being released for sale. They are rich red in colour.

Tawny ports are sweet or medium dry and start off as ruby port. The wine is aged for at least seven years in wooden barrels and during that time gradually oxidises changing colour to golden-brown – hence the name.

White ports are made with white grapes and vary in style from very dry to semi-sweet. Like ruby port they are usually consumed young. When they mature for long periods, the colour darkens and they resemble tawny port.

Vintage port is made from grapes of one year's harvest. The wine is aged in barrels for a maximum of two and a half years before bottling. This unfiltered wine matures in the bottle for ten to thirty years before being considered ready for drinking. It should not be mistaken for Late Bottled Vintage which is aged in wood for four to six years before being filtered, bottled and sold.

TYPES OF SHERRY

Here's a test – go to the cupboard and look to see if there is a dusty old crusted bottle of cooking sherry. If so, when the Spanish Inquisition comes for tea do not admit what is lurking in the darkness of the pantry. Instead start throwing around words like 'fino' – that should guarantee safety.

Sherry comes in a variety of categories and styles – dry, sweet, cream and blended.

Fino is pale, bone dry, light and fragrant. In Spanish the word *fino* means fine and this delicate sherry lives up to its name.

Manzanilla is dry with a fresh acidity. The word *manzanilla* means 'little apple' in Spanish which with the sherry's tangy fruity character may explain the moniker.

Oloroso is a rich, amber medium sweet sherry and as the name suggests (it means scented) is aromatic.

Amontillado is named after the region of Montilla. This sherry is medium dry with a nutty character somewhere between fino and oloroso.

Cream sherry is the most popular style of sherry outside Spain, and in Britain would be known as old lady or cooking sherry. It is sweetened usually with concentrated grape juice or in better quality brands, by blending with the naturally sweet Pedro Ximenez sherry. Pale cream is made with fino, and cream sherry with a base of oloroso.

Pedro Ximenez or PX is named after the white grape variety. It makes intensely sweet dark sherry that is normally sipped with dessert.

HOW TO MAKE SHERRY

Sherry is made with a dry white wine base to which distilled grape spirit is added after fermentation. Before fortification the wine is tasted for quality and the producer will decide which variety of sherry it is destined to become. This classification dictates what happens next. If the sherry is to be fino or manzanilla then before it is transferred to wooden casks for aging it receives a dose of spirit of a low-enough ABV that the development of a layer of yeast called flor will not be hampered. Flor acts as a protective blanket that shields against oxygen, lowers acidity, and maintains a fresh taste and pale colour. For oloroso, amontillado and Pedro Ximenez, oxidisation is welcomed as the sherry becomes a darker shade and characteristic nutty, caramel flavours develop. These types of sherry are not to be matured under flor so they are fortified to a higher alcohol level to prevent yeast from growing.

Sherry is aged using the *solera* system. This is a collection of wooden casks that contain wines from a variety of years. Younger wines are blended with older wines because each time the wine in the oldest cask is partially tapped for bottling, it is refilled with wine from the second oldest cask. That one is then topped up with wine from the third oldest, and so on all the way back to the youngest cask which is filled with newly made wine. None of the casks is ever drained completely so the blending of young and old wines is a continual process.

By law, a wine can only be called sherry if it is made in the triangle encompassing the towns of Jerez de la Frontera, Sanlúcar de Barrameda and El Puerto de Santa Maria in the Spanish region of Andalusia.

HOW TO MAKE MADEIRA

Madeira is made by fermenting grape juice. During fermentation grape spirit is added and this stops the action of the yeast, leaving unfermented sugars in the wine and giving Madeira its characteristic sweetness. It then goes through a unique process called *estufagem* (from the Portuguese and Spanish word *estufa* for oven or kiln). This entails heating the wine up to 60 °C and deliberately exposing it to air so it oxidises and imparts a distinctive flavour and dark colour. The tradition began when a batch of Madeira had been returned to the islands after months on board a ship. During the voyage the effects of temperature change on the barrels as the ship crossed the equator and the movement of the ocean had transformed the wine for the better. Wines described as *vinho da roda* (wines that have made a round trip) became popular but it was an expensive production method and so vintners experimented to find the best ways to replicate the action of heat and waves. They tried storing barrels in rooms where the sun's heat would affect the wine. It worked and imbued the wine with the desired characteristics of *vinho da roda*. Nowadays depending on the value of the Madeira it is heated in stainless steel or concrete tanks surrounded by heating coils (for cheaper quality); aged in wooden casks for up to a year in a sauna-like room heated by steam; or for the highest-quality wine the barrels are left to age for decades in the sun's heat.

VERMOUTH

Vermouth is fortified wine infused with aromatic herbs and spices and comes in dry, medium dry, and sweet varieties. Its name derives from the German word for wormwood *wermut* (or in old German *wermuth*) inspired by the plant's bitter undertones. Vermouth was first documented in Italy in the mid-sixteenth century and the fashion for drinking it spread throughout Europe as *wermut wein* in Germany and in France as *vermouth*. Where would drinkers of Martini or manhattan cocktails be without it?

STRIP ME NAKED – GIN

Buy a snifter for the Victorian PR genius (unknown) who changed the reputation of gin from the Devil's drink to the botanical stalwart of the drinks cabinet. It's hard to believe now when one looks at the proliferation of stylish brands that gin was known in eighteenth-century Britain as Strip me Naked, Kill me Quick, Madame Geneva, Blue Ruin, Cobbler's Punch, Crank, Drain, Diddle, Frogs' Wine, Lightning, Rag Water, and Mother's Ruin amongst other derogatory nicknames. This was a period known as the Gin Craze when at its peak in 1743 the annual per capita consumption was 2.2 gallons. But consider this – most people in the countryside drank beer or cider not gin so 2.2 gallons does not give an accurate picture of how much city dwellers were drinking. In London it was estimated to be an astonishing fourteen gallons per year for each adult male.

Gin's nickname Mother's Ruin was based in truth because gin misuse rendered women sterile and caused impotence in men – two reasons why the birth rate in London was exceeded by the death rate. Gin was responsible for an increase in mortality that slowed London's growing population. Nowadays it would be called death by misadventure but then it was death by Kill me Quick when people slumped paralytic in the street were trampled by horses, froze to death, or were so out of it they fell in the river and drowned.

What explains this frenzy for such destructive drink? There are several factors – water was polluted so people drank gin instead; life for many urban dwellers was miserable – they lived in dreadful conditions in utter poverty so gin was a swift route to oblivion; it was widely available; but more than anything it was cheap. That was an unintended consequence when in 1690 'An Act for Encouraging of the Distillation of Brandy and Spirits from Corn' was passed in order to raise funds for the Exchequer and to create demand for a glut of cereals grown on the estates of powerful landowners, many of whom were parliamentarians. As long as a licence was purchased anyone could legally distil alcohol with English grain. And distil it they did, creating such huge supply and demand that the price of a glass of gin was sometimes lower than that of beer. By the eighteenth century in London, a city of less than one million people, there were 7,000 places to buy gin – blacksmiths, private houses, on the street, in church crypts, even inside prisons. No wonder one commentator noted that 'Drunkenness of the common people was universal, the whole town of London swarmed with drunken people from morning till night'. For a contemporaneous image of a typical eighteenth-century slum scene see William Hogarth's *Gin Lane* which illustrates the misery, madness and devastation of what writer Tobias Smollet described as a 'mischievous potion'. A poem written around the same time by the Reverend James Townley compared evil gin with benign beer:

> *Gin cursed fiend with fury fraught*
> *Makes human race a prey*
> *It enters by a deadly draught*
> *And steals our life away.*

> *Beer! Happy produce of our isle*
> *Can sinewy strength impart*
> *And wearied with fatigue and toil*
> *Can cheer each manly heart.*

What would the doctor credited with inventing gin have thought?

Physician Franciscus Sylvius known as Franz de la Boë, was professor of medicine at the University of Leyden, Holland, and in 1650 he created an elixir from distilled malted cereal that he flavoured with juniper. He called it *genever* after the Dutch word for juniper and used it on his patients to treat gallstones, stomach and kidney ailments and gout. But Dr Sylvius was not the first to use juniper in spirit. Eleventh-century Italian monks experimented with distilled wine flavoured with juniper as a remedy for a number of ailments including plague. It did not work for the plague but people were still happy to give it a go.

Genever (from where the word 'gin' and the nickname Madame Geneva stem) grew in popularity in England with a confluence of historical events. Protestant Dutch prince, William of Orange, was invited by a group of English politicians to overthrow the unpopular King James II and take the throne in a dual monarchy with James's daughter Mary (who was married to William). James II fled to France and so the never-ending conflict between England and France was reignited and in the subsequent 126 years six wars were prosecuted with the old enemy, which drained English coffers. If only there was something with a constant demand that could be taxed... The Dutch connection meant increased imports from William's homeland including genever so the English soon gained a taste for 'strong water'. When the import of brandy from France was banned it left drinkers with little option for hard liquor. Government policy to encourage distilling resulted in an underclass of city dwellers that were permanently blathered with the associated problems of crime, depravity, and reduced productivity. In an effort to rebottle the genie, eight Gin Acts were passed in the years 1729–1751 but they had little effect on

Genever (also spelled jenever) is still consumed in the Netherlands and is a distinctly different drink to London or Plymouth gin. It has a pronounced malty character. Unlike gin which is mostly consumed with a mixer, genever is served neat the way that schnapps or aquavit is in Scandinavia.

A sloe is the fruit of the blackthorn bush and when infused with gin and sugar for at least three months it turns into a ruby-coloured liqueur with a rich fruity flavour. Traditionally each berry should be pricked with a thorn from the bush on which they were picked.

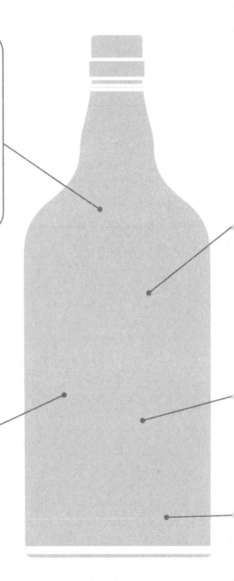

Next time someone uses the 'for medicinal purposes only' excuse, give a thought to gin and tonic which was originally consumed as medicine. During the early days of the British Empire colonists took extract of quinine bark for its anti-malarial properties. To make quinine easier to consume it was dissolved in carbonated water. Johann Schweppe invented the world's first mass-produced soft drink – Indian tonic water – in 1771, but the quinine still tasted nasty; so what to do? Why not add gin and the botanicals would mask the taste of the drug. What was to become one of the world's most popular cocktails started out as just what the doctor ordered.

Plymouth gin is fruitier, more aromatic and fuller bodied than its London counterpart. It is made in the medieval Black Friars Distillery, a former monastery in Plymouth. This site is notable for being not only the one place this type of gin is produced, but also where in 1620 the Pilgrim Fathers spent their last night in England before boarding the *Mayflower* ship on their voyage to America.

The nineteenth-century temperance movement targeted women and tried to persuade them to give up the demon drink. After all 'Little nips of whisky, little drops of gin, make a lady wonder where on earth she's bin'.

Bathtub gin is any style of homemade spirit and usually refers to the poor-quality secretly produced hooch that proliferated in the USA during Prohibition. It was not made in a bathtub as the name implies, rather the bottles it came in were topped up with water from a bath tap or sink. Such rough-tasting spirit needed disguising and so cocktails really came into their own with fruit and herbs added to make them more palatable.

London dry gin is a specific premium style of gin that must by law be produced by redistilling ethyl alcohol with natural botanicals that aromatise and flavour the spirit during the distillation process and not after. No artificial ingredients may be used and apart from a tiny amount of sugar to sweeten the spirit the only extra substance that may be added is water.

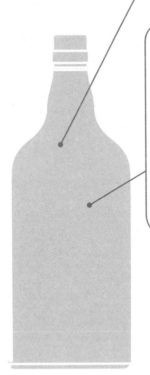

consumption. What did influence a decline in sales of gin was a combination of bad harvests, population growth, a reduction in wages and an increase in the prices of both food and gin. Most poor people could not afford it any more. The worst of the gin frenzy might have been over but gin did not go away completely. Charles Dickens documented society as he saw it and in nineteenth-century London gin was still a scourge of the poor. As he wrote in the *Evening Chronicle* in 1835:

> *Gin-drinking is a great vice in England, but wretchedness and dirt are a greater; and until you improve the homes of the poor, or persuade a half-famished wretch not to seek relief in the temporary oblivion of his own misery, with the pittance which, divided among his family, would furnish a morsel of bread for each, gin-shops will increase in number and splendour.*

So how did gin become respectable? It started when British naval ships started carrying gin for sailors' rations. Lime was added to prevent scurvy and – voila! – the gimlet (which may have been named after the tool used for drilling holes in barrels of lime juice). Not only was that cocktail born on the high seas but pink gin was too – a potation which acquired its colour from bitters issued to sailors as a remedy for seasickness. But the most significant development in the rehabilitation of gin was British colonists in India and other malaria-rampant countries who brought home the habit of drinking G&T. By the time cocktails became de rigeur in the early twentieth century, gin was in. Now with the renaissance of gin distilling and a plethora of luxury boutique brands, Madame Geneva has moved from the gutter into the pantheon of perfect spirits.

When in 1737 the British parliament passed a law to reward informers for reporting unlicensed gin sellers, subterfuge by the vendors was required. They invented a way of selling the illicit booze that required the passwords 'puss' and 'mew'. These may have stemmed from one of the nicknames of gin – Old Tom. Exactly how it worked is not clear as research sources cite a number of explanations. It may have been one of these:

- A vendor in a house concealed behind a curtain or board responded to a buyer's query 'puss' by replying 'mew'. When the buyer dropped payment into a drawer that slid in and out from the curtain, the vendor handed over a dram of gin.

- When buyers saw the outline of a cat drawn on the door or window of a house they whispered 'puss'. If the response was 'mew' they deposited coins through the mouth of the cat and a measure of gin was poured through a pipe protruding from the cat's tail.

This method proliferated in London for a few months until the informants got wind of it.

HOW TO MAKE GIN

Gin is distilled spirit alcohol made from fermented malted cereal such as barley, wheat, and corn; or potatoes and sugar cane. The neutral spirit is redistilled so the alcoholic vapours pass through a basket of botanicals in the still and receive their aromas and flavours. Without the botanicals gin would have little or no flavour. The principal ingredient is juniper berries sourced from a species of coniferous tree. Individual gin makers have their own secret recipes and typically a premium gin will contain up to ten plants such as coriander, angelica, orange peel, lemon peel, saffron, cardamom, cinnamon, and nutmeg. Purified water dilutes the concentrated gin down to a minimum strength of 37.5 per cent ABV.

MYTHICAL MEAD

Mead may have been the first alcoholic drink purposely made by humans at least 20,000 years ago. Wild honey was widely available and mead would have been simple to produce – add water to honey and wait for a few days for wild yeast to ferment the sugars.

The term mead derives from Old English *meodu* which might originally have stemmed from a Sanskrit word for sweet – *madhu*. It has mythical associations not least because it was mentioned in the epic poem *Beowulf* where the eponymous hero battles the troll-like Grendel in a mead hall; and in Norse mythology where dead Viking warriors in Valhalla drank mead from the udder of the goat Heidrun served up in the skulls of their enemies. Vikings in real life were binge drinkers and alcohol was central to their culture. They drank ale, wine and mead in special drinking chambers called mead halls. Feuds were often settled by fighting or burning down the hall with the enemy inside. Warriors known as berserkers drank heavily before battle until so furious they became uncontrollable psychopaths with no fear.

Mead halls were central to the culture of other northern European peoples including the Anglo-Saxons. Each community had one and they were venues where men gathered to drink, listen to stories, sing, declare their allegiances and strengthen bonds. They were male-dominated venues where women acted as cupbearers to pass the communal drinking horns or wooden vessels around the group. Those women were known as Weavers of Peace because the female presence helped to calm raging testosterone. A drinking ceremony known today as the Loving Cup helped to maintain friendships. In this ritual a group

When the tomb of King Midas was excavated in central Turkey in 1957 archaeologists discovered 150 bronze drinking vessels dating to circa 730 BC. Residue in the containers consisted of fermented honey, barley, grapes, and spices. Remains of organic material also found in the tomb led to the conclusion that it was a funerary feast. Mourners had eaten lentil and lamb stew washed down by a spicy pyment/beer hybrid at Midas's funeral.

assembles in a circle. Three people stand up at the same time, one to pass the cup, one to drink from it, and the third to 'defend'. In previous centuries the defender would have drawn his sword or axe ready to guard the back of the drinker who was vulnerable to attack as he took a sip. The cup is wiped clean and passed to the defender as the person next to him stands to become the guard and so on it goes around the company until everyone has supped from the Loving Cup.

Why mead eventually went out of fashion is a mystery. Perhaps when sugar became so easily available from plantations in the New World there was an alternative to the sweetness mead had previously supplied. Tastes may also have changed in the eleventh century when hops started to be used in brewing beer, shifting preferences from sweet to bitter.

One place that keeps the tradition of mead alive is Holy Island a.k.a. Lindisfarne off the coast of Northumberland. St Aiden arrived on the island in AD 635 and founded a monastery. Today's mead is made in St Aiden's winery although technically it is a version of the drink called pyment – white grape wine sweetened with honey and flavoured with herbs – known in ancient Rome as *mulsum*. It is sweet enough to pass as a dessert wine. Other types of mead are melomel – with fermented fruit; cyser – fermented apple juice and honey; and metheglin is a spiced variety.

EXCOMMUNICATION – MEZCAL AND TEQUILA

Picture the scene – a first-century sun-baked Mexican desert scape where only cacti and other xerophytic vegetation can grow. You're parched and could really do with a drink. You look around and notice a spiky succulent plant called agave, a.k.a. maguey, and remember the saying 'when life hands you a lemon, make lemonade'. So you take the pulp from the stalk and press the juice from it. In the heat it does not take long for the sugars to ferment and turn into a mildly alcoholic drink. Mmmm tasty. News of this discovery spreads and agave give up their treasure to make a libation known as *octili poliqhui*, a sacred drink that gave 'delight for the gods and priests'.

When the Spanish invaded Mexico in the early sixteenth century they shortened *octili poliqhui* to *pulque* (poolkay). But *pulque* was too bland for the conquistadors and after their supplies of brandy from home ran out they tried distilling it. The resulting *aguardiente*, or fire water, was not satisfying initially and potions nicknamed 'excommunication' and 'cock's eye' put hairs on the chest. But with experimentation and the discovery that if the agave stalks were baked before fermenting, the pulp was much sweeter, this *aguamiel*, or honey water, was made into 'mezcal wine' which when distilled became very popular with the natives. The name mezcal derives from the Nahuatl language *mezcalli*, where *metl* = agave and *ixcalli* = cooked.

All tequila is mezcal, but not all mezcal is tequila. Tequila is named after the town of that name in Jalisco state and to qualify as genuine it must be

In 2009 a Mexican scientist turned alchemist heated a shot of tequila to 800 °C with an unexpected result. As the tequila vaporised, its molecular structure split into atomic constituents and a fine layer of carbon was produced. When examined under a microscope he discovered that the carbon had formed into thousands of structures identical to diamonds. As each one had a diameter of only one thousandth of a millimetre, they would not end up in an engagement ring, but might have an application as semiconductors in electronic circuits.

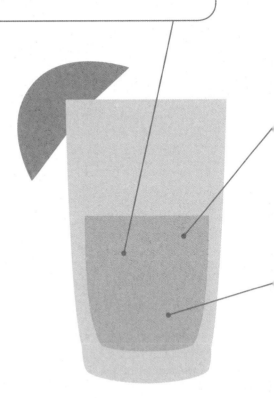

Some bottles of mezcal contain what looks like a worm. It is actually the pickled larva of either the *Hypopta agavis* moth or the agave snout weevil. The grub has a reputation (erroneous) for causing hallucinations – this may be because mezcal sounds like mescaline, a psychedelic drug. Addition of larvae started in 1950 as a marketing gimmick with the claim that they enhanced the flavour of the spirit. There could be truth in this because meat added during the production of alcoholic drinks is not new. Mezcal producers in previous centuries often threw a chicken into the vat for extra richness.

Try eating the grub fried and ground up with chilli. In Oaxaca it is a delicacy with medicinal properties. Take a pinch of grub and place it on the tongue then slowly sip the mezcal, straight, not in a cocktail. Now repeat.

Pulque known as the 'elixir of the gods' had mythical origins when, the legend goes, an agave plant was struck by a lightning bolt causing it to split open and release the fermented juice. Agave was so important to Aztecs that they had an agave goddess, Mayahuel. There were strict rules associated with the making and consumption of *pulque*. Brewers would eschew sex during production to avoid souring the brew. It had such ritual significance that drinking *pulque* in everyday life was considered to be sacrilegious for a section of the populous. The masses were restricted to drinking it only on certain feast days, although the elders (over the age of fifty-two years), the elite, and warriors could indulge freely as recognition of their exalted place in society. Anyone else caught drinking during forbidden periods was punished. The lightest sanction was to have their hair shorn, the worst was execution.

made from a specific type of agave (blue) in the municipalities of Tequila or Arandas.

Tequila is produced in huge batches on a commercial scale whereas most mezcal is made slowly in small distilleries in a hand-crafted manner that adds more individuality to the finished product. Wild agaves are often harvested for use in mezcal and like wine with *terroir*, the differences in soil and other local factors influence the taste of the spirit.

Tequila and mezcal's reputation grew when Mexico's giant northern neighbour passed the National Prohibition Act in 1919 and thirsty Americans started to cross the border from California and Texas in search of hooch. But it was the margarita that really did it. Tequila, or mezcal, orange liqueur and lime juice with a salty glass rim served on the rocks or blended with ice became America's favourite cocktail. Like many alcohol-related subjects there are a number of theories about who made it first and where. One plausible story is that the margarita is a version of an American drink called the 'daisy' made in Mexico with tequila rather than brandy. The Spanish translation of 'daisy' is margarita.

Tequila is one of those spirits that inspire profound horror and flashbacks in people who have overindulged. It has the status of being the ultimate party bevvy where the theatre of drinking it is more important than the taste. Outside Mexico this means tequila slammers where salt is licked, the shot is downed in one, and a slice of lime sucked all the while as the rest of the group cheer. Guaranteed to cause a *muy grande cruda*!

HOW TO MAKE MEZCAL

Cut the bulbous agave *piña* from its root and slice it into quarters. For tequila these are cooked for a few hours in a huge pressure cooker, for mezcal they are baked for several days in an underground oven heated with wood charcoal that gives them a distinct smoky flavour. With traditional mezcal the baked agave is crushed by a stone wheel pulled by a mule through a stone trough. Heating the agave begins the conversion of starch to sugar ready for it to be fermented in water in large vats or barrels – tequila with cultured yeast and mezcal with wild yeast. After fermentation the brew is boiled and the alcohol distilled.

For everyday brands, the liquor is bottled without being aged. Caramel, prune juice or sherry is added for colour and to take the edge off the hard spirit. If it is destined to be *reposado* (rested) the spirit is aged in wood for up to nine months. *Añejo* (old) is matured for up to four years in oak casks – often used American bourbon barrels.

KILL DEVIL – RUM

'A hot, hellish and terrible liquor'
is how rum was first described in
writing in 1651. No wonder it had
the nickname Kill Devil. Rum was first
distilled in Barbados in the mid-seventeenth
century when someone discovered that
molasses added to water could be fermented
and then distilled. Until then they were a worthless
by-product of the sugar industry used as fertiliser or pig
feed. The etymology of the term rum is not clear. Other names
for it were rumbullion and rumbustion, both English slang terms
meaning 'uproar' or 'brawl'. The Latin name for sugar cane is
Saccharum officinarum so that also sounds plausible as the origin.

The history of rum is the history of sugar and consequently
it is connected with slavery in the New World. Christopher
Columbus transported sugar cane plants to Hispaniola in 1493
and Portuguese explorers took them to Brazil around the same
time. The Caribbean had a perfect climate for growing sugar
cane. All the leading maritime powers, Spain, France,
Holland, Portugal and England, established hundreds
of sugar plantations, built processing mills, and
installed distilling equipment to process an
endlessly in-demand commodity. Such a vast

industry required labour so enslaved Africans were trafficked across the Atlantic to work the land. Rum became an internationally celebrated drink when it was sold to passing ships, spreading its reputation and creating a thriving export market.

When molasses were shipped from the Caribbean to distilleries in New England the slavery triangle was completed. Rum was exported to Africa in exchange for human cargo to sell to owners of sugar plantations. Slavers in Africa started accepting rum as preferred payment and business could not be conducted without it. Rum could even be bartered for gold. In addition to being consumed socially alcohol was widely used in Africa to mark rites of passage (birth, puberty, death), and it was offered as a sacrifice to local deities. It has been estimated that between 1680 and 1713 approximately 1.3 million gallons of rum were shipped to Africa from the Americas and swapped for up to 60,000 slaves to toil on plantations.

In New England rum became the drink of choice and it had such importance that a contract was not sealed until a glass had been supped. Anyone who reneged on a deal had to provide as compensation a gallon of rum or a half barrel of beer to the injured party. Fur traders depended on rum (and brandy) when buying skins from Native Americans and they got better deals if booze was included in the payment. Initially the American colonists imported rum from the Caribbean – quite often from French-controlled sugar islands and that was beyond the pale for their political masters back in London. Supporting the French enemy was intolerable so Britain passed the Sugar Act in 1764 (a.k.a. the American Revenue Act) with the intention of taxing rum, molasses and Madeira wine imported into the colony. Such interference from parliamentarians thousands of miles away did nothing to support deteriorating relations and it confirmed to the colonists why they wanted freedom from the mother country. No taxation without representation. Twelve years later the Declaration of Independence was issued. American Founding Father John Adams said 'I know not why we should blush to confess that molasses was an essential ingredient in American independence'. So it was not about tea after all, it was rum wot did it.

HOW RUM IS MADE

Rum is made by fermenting sugar cane juice or molasses and water with cultured or airborne wild yeasts then distilling it. Rum comes out of the still as clear, colourless spirit and the addition of caramel or length of time ageing in an oak barrel will determine the colour and the richness of the flavour. Spiced rums are infused with spices after fermentation.

Imagine the shopping list of the First Fleet as it planned the journey to establish the Australian penal colony in Botany Bay, Sydney. Eleven ships left Britain in 1787 carrying just over a thousand people, the majority convicts. The fleet stopped three times throughout the journey to pick up supplies and alcohol was the priority. In the Canary Islands and Cape Town wine was acquired and rum too in Rio de Janeiro – enough for three years' supply – slightly more than the two years' stash of food on board. A supply of rum was essential as the soldiers guarding the convicts were entitled to half a pint per day. British supply ships came from Bengal and Cape Town and because the colonists were dependent on unreliable deliveries of imported goods, prices were extortionate. The most valuable commodity was booze and it became an unofficial currency that could buy anything including labour. But as drink was prized above anything else some workers would trade their time much more cheaply when compensated in alcohol than they would have done in monetary form so eventually it had a detrimental effect on the economy.

Drunkenness in the new colony was rife and whoever controlled the supply of liquor had the power. This was a group of New South Wales soldiers known as the Rum Corps who had the monopoly on importation of spirits. The colony's governor was unable to contain the corruption so tough measures were required and this meant replacing him with someone with a big reputation – Captain William Bligh of the *Bounty* ship infamy. Bligh arrived in 1806 with instructions to regulate the trade and eliminate the scourge of inebriation. This thankless task was made no easier by Bligh's brusque manner, which did not endear him to the locals. For the second time in Captain Bligh's career his subordinates mutinied as the Rum Corps arrested him and installed one of their officers in his place. Australia's first and only military coup was known initially as the Great Rebellion and later the Rum Rebellion.

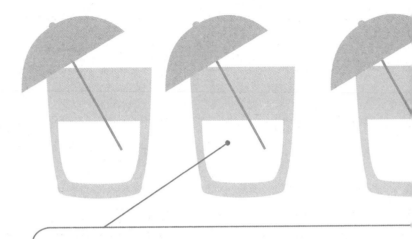

Rum became a substitute for French brandy on British Royal Navy ships soon after Jamaica was captured from Spain in 1655, and a regular supply of rum was readily available. Originally the ration was downed neat but when in 1740 Admiral Edward Vernon suggested diluting it by adding water and lime juice, it gave His Majesty's sailors a health advantage because lime juice contained vitamin C and prevented them suffering from scurvy. The drink became known as 'grog'; named after Vernon himself as he was already called 'Old Grogram' by his men from his habit of wearing a distinctive grogram coat. Spanish sailors' alcohol rations were wine or sherry, French sailors received wine or *eau de vie*, none of which contained essential vitamins. Grog also meant that British sailors were less likely to fall prey to the intoxicating effects of their daily one pint of high-alcohol rum. Vernon described the rum problem this way: 'The pernicious custom of the seamen drinking their allowance of rum in drams and often at once is attended with many fatal consequences to their morals as well as their health. Many of their lives shortened thereby... besides stupefying their rational qualities which makes them heedlessly slaves to every brutish passion.'

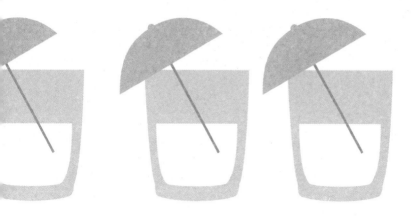

Naval personnel continued to receive a rum ration, albeit a dram rather than a pint, until 1970 when on a date known in the Royal Navy as Black Tot Day the tradition was ended. Sailors wore black armbands and toasted the monarch for the last time after which the empty glasses were thrown overboard to be buried at sea. Today a rum tot is still issued on special occasions by instruction of the Queen or a senior member of the Royal Family. On such days the euphemism 'splice the mainbrace' is employed. An extra rum ration was historically issued to sailors who completed the tricky task of fixing part of the rigging called the mainbrace. In Diamond Jubilee year 2012 the Queen sent a message to the navy: 'Please convey my warm thanks to all those who serve in the Royal Navy for their kind message of loyal greetings sent on the occasion of my official birthday and the 60th anniversary of my accession to the throne. In this Diamond Jubilee year, Prince Philip and I send our good wishes to you all. Splice the mainbrace. Elizabeth R.'

Think rum, think **Caribbean,** because almost all major islands produce a distinctive style:

- **Barbados** is where rum distillation began. Mount Gay Distillery dates to 1663 and is the world's oldest operating rum producer.
- **Cuba** is best known for white rum.
- **Dominican Republic** is renowned for full-bodied, aged rum.
- **Guyana** produces rich, heavy Demerara rums named after a local river.
- **Haiti** makes heavier rums and specialises in illicit moonshine for use in voodoo rituals.
- **Jamaica** is celebrated for rich, aromatic rum.
- **Puerto Rico** is known for light, dry rums.
- **Trinidad** produces mainly light rum.

Other countries that produce rum include Guatemala, Nicaragua, Brazil, Venezuela, USA, Canada, Australia, Tahiti, Thailand, and the Philippines.

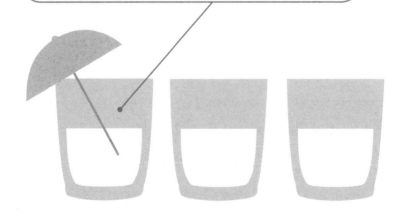

During the First World War, British soldiers on the front line received one-eighth of a pint of rum per day. It was decanted from gallon-sized cream earthenware flagons marked SRD (Supply Reserve Depot) or as the soldiers nicknamed it 'Seldom Reaches Destination' or 'Soon Runs Dry'. Thousands of used flagons littered the battlefields after the war and they are now a collectors' item. It was also used as a purgative if soldiers had been gassed – they were force-fed huge amounts of rum until they vomited – with the intention of expelling the poisonous gas at the same time.

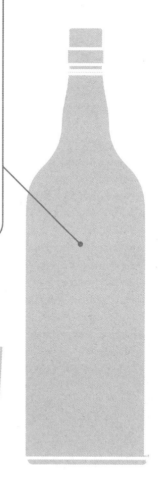

WHERE'S THE PARTY? – SPARKLING WINE

Pop the cork and the party begins. Sparkling wine has a unique ability to create anticipation and lighten the mood. Commonly known by the name 'champagne' regardless of where it is produced, fizz can only legally use that name if the grapes are grown and the wine made according to the rules of *appellation* in the French region of Champagne. French sparkling wines made in other parts of the country are known as *crémant* or *mousseux*.

Britons are the second most enthusiastic drinkers of champers after the French and with good reason. Sparkling wine made through secondary fermentation in the bottle may first have happened in England not France, albeit with imported French still wine. Although Dom Pierre Pérignon (*c*.1638–1715) has been credited with the invention of sparkling wine, it is not true. He *was* a winemaker and expert cellarman based at the Abbey de Hautvillers in the Champagne region and he worked to improve local wines and viticulture – but the credit for fizz belongs elsewhere. Sparkling wine was known by Dom Pérignon, but for many years fizzy wine was seen as a fault that caused bottles to break and create a chain reaction in the caves leading to its description as *le vin du diable* – the Devil's wine. The erroneous champagne invention myth may have arisen because of an account written by a priest called Dom Groussard more than a century after Dom Pérignon's death, in which he claimed the latter was the inventor of champagne. By then leading champagne houses such as Taittinger and Veuve Clicquot had been founded and were a source of national pride so perhaps Dom Groussard

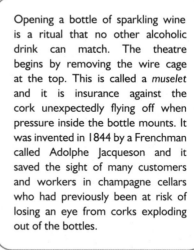

Opening a bottle of sparkling wine is a ritual that no other alcoholic drink can match. The theatre begins by removing the wire cage at the top. This is called a *muselet* and it is insurance against the cork unexpectedly flying off when pressure inside the bottle mounts. It was invented in 1844 by a Frenchman called Adolphe Jacqueson and it saved the sight of many customers and workers in champagne cellars who had previously been at risk of losing an eye from corks exploding out of the bottles.

Some people swear that hanging a spoon in an open bottle of sparkling wine maintains the fizz. Scientific experiments have proved that the spoon has no effect. Perhaps people are not aware how long it takes sparkling wine to lose its fizz so when they return to it the following day and it still has a slight tingle they assume it is the spoon's influence.

Winston Churchill's morning tea break consisted not of a cup of *Camellia sinensis* but a glass (large) of champagne brought by his valet every day at 11 a.m. He is quoted as saying 'A single glass of champagne imparts a feeling of exhilaration. The nerves are braced, the imagination is agreeably stirred, the wits become more nimble.' Churchill's favourite brand was Pol Roger and he maintained a stash during the Second World War, even though the Champagne region was occupied by the Nazis. When he died, as a mark of respect to their celebrated client Pol Roger added a black border to the labels of 'White Foil' sold in Britain.

Sabrage is a ceremonial method of opening a bottle of champagne by using a heavy knife or special sword (*sabre à champagne*) to cut open the top rather than pop the cork. The force of the blade makes a clean cut at the weakest part of the bottle on the neck just underneath the cork. It is not the sharpness of the blade that counts, rather the weight. Pressure inside ensures that no glass shards fall into the bottle.

One theory about the origin of the practice is that cavalry solders in Napoleon's army used their swords to whisk the top off the bottle rather than dismount and open it by removing the cork.

In the 1800s champagne was noticeably sweeter than the modern version is. The trend towards a drier product began when Perrier-Jouët decided not to sweeten the 1846 vintage prior to exporting it to London. The designation *brut* was created for the British market in 1876.

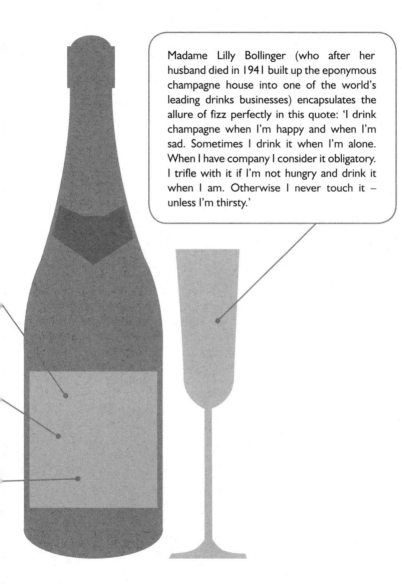

Madame Lilly Bollinger (who after her husband died in 1941 built up the eponymous champagne house into one of the world's leading drinks businesses) encapsulates the allure of fizz perfectly in this quote: 'I drink champagne when I'm happy and when I'm sad. Sometimes I drink it when I'm alone. When I have company I consider it obligatory. I trifle with it if I'm not hungry and drink it when I am. Otherwise I never touch it – unless I'm thirsty.'

Making champagne was a dangerous business until French glassmakers perfected their own version of *verre anglais*. Until then it was common for bottles to smash during the secondary fermentation, especially in warm weather. Flying glass badly injured people working in the cellars and so they were issued with protective clothing including metal masks.

Why do racing drivers waste all that champagne by spraying it willy-nilly to celebrate a win? Blame an American motorsport driver called Dan Gurney who spontaneously doused his team mates on the podium after he won the Le Mans race in 1967. Other drivers followed suit and soon it became tradition. When Formula I races are held in Muslim countries (where alcohol is forbidden) the champers is switched to *waard*, which is a fizzy soft drink made from rose water and pomegranate.

wanted to aggrandise Abbey de Hautvillers with his claims. Moët et Chandon must have believed it because they named their premier brand after Dom Pérignon.

England's connection with this marvellous creation is documented in a paper called *Some Observations concerning the Ordering of Wines* delivered in 1662 (six years before Dom Pérignon entered the abbey) by scientist Christopher Merret (also spelled Merrett) to the Royal Society in London. In it he described how 'our wine coopers of recent times use vast quantities of sugar and molasses to all sorts of wine to make them brisk and sparkling'. Six months later, cider maker Silas Taylor presented a paper to the Royal Society where he described bottling cider and keeping it in cool water, which made it 'drink quick and lively, it comes into the glass not pale or troubled but bright yellow, with a speedy vanishing nittiness (meaning full of small air bubbles)... which evaporates with a sparkling and whizzing noise.' It was already known that cider makers had added sugar to cider around 1632, before Dom Pérignon was born, so Silas Taylor was describing sparkling cider in his paper. Doing the same to wine was an obvious move.

Secondary fermentation of wine was not new. It often happened naturally in warm weather when yeast awoke and started fermenting residual sugars creating carbon dioxide bubbles. The problem was that carbon dioxide creates pressure in an enclosed container so whatever vessel wine or cider was stored in would need to be hardy enough to withstand the force. This is where England's claim to have intentionally created sparkling wine is bolstered and it is linked to three seventeenth-century glass-makers. James Howell and Sir Robert Mansel perfected a technique to make coal-fired glassware reinforced with iron and manganese ores making it more resilient than any other existing

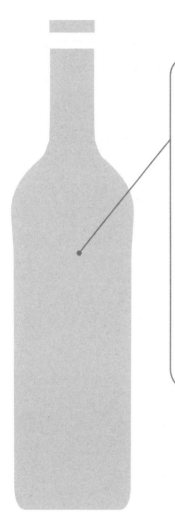

A bottle of fizz contains around 100 million bubbles. Primarily made up of carbon dioxide, the bubbles do more than just tickle the nose; they also enhance the wine by picking up flavour and aroma on their ascent to explode at the surface. They contain up to thirty times more flavour-enhancing chemicals than the rest of the wine, so the more effervescence the better. For bubbles to develop most effectively they need a nucleation point – a small defect in the glass that traps vibrating dissolved carbon dioxide. This forms into a bubble that is expelled, its place immediately taken by more gas and so on until strings of bubbles are visible to the eye as they break away and rise to the surface.

Champagne Veuve Clicquot Ponsardin goes by the nickname 'the widow' (which is the English translation of 'veuve'). When Francois Clicquot died in 1805 his wife Barbe-Nicole Ponsardin took control of the company and built it into one of the world's leading luxury brands. Madame Clicquot is also credited with inventing the practice of *dégorgement* in 1818.

A big selling point for champagne is the pop of the bottle and the fizz. This makes the wine swiftly go to the head. Carbonation speeds up the rate of intoxication as the bubbles open the pyloric sphincter (the valve that releases the stomach's content) sending alcohol into the small intestine where it is absorbed into the bloodstream. Glassware also has an effect – a flute maintains the bubbles whereas a shallow coupe dissipates them.

Which shape of glass is best? Three glass shapes are commonly used for sparkling wine but which is best – flute, coupe or tulip? That's up to the person holding it.

A flute has a long stem, narrow straight sides, and a small nucleation point where the bubbles form. The shape helps to retain the bubbles permitting them to rise gracefully to the rim. This is very important as they carry aroma and flavour and enhance the enjoyment.

A coupe is a shallow glass with a broad bowl, also known as a champagne saucer. The legend that it was modelled on the breast shape of either Empress Josephine, Marie Antoinette or Madame de Pompadour is a myth as it was already in use in England before all these women were born. Champagne served in a coupe loses its carbonation quickly and what is fizz without bubbles?

A tulip in which the rim is narrower than the belly of the glass will deliver more aroma to the drinker than a flute and the shape will not cause the champers to lose carbonation too quickly.

glass. Glassworks were set up in major ports where wine imported in casks could be decanted into the new heavy-duty glass bottles. Sir Kenelm Digby also experimented in glass-making by adding high ratios of lime and potash. The result, *verre anglais*, was robust and like Howell and Mansel's glass could withstand the carbon dioxide pressure from cider and wine undergoing a secondary fermentation in the bottle. But having a sturdy bottle is not much use unless it can be sealed. Kenelm Digby is credited as being the first person in England to use leak-proof corks to seal bottles. England had long-standing trade connections with Portugal where cork oaks grow. Until 1685 French winemakers used a plug of wood wrapped in fabric and soaked in tallow rather than a cork to seal the bottle. Such devices would not have prevented carbon dioxide leakage and so the wine would no longer have sparkled. This factor is another reason to suggest that sparkling wine was not a French innovation.

England's winemaking history dates back at least to the Norman Conquest in 1066 although today's yields will not give French or Italian vintners sleepless nights. The undisputed champ of English vino is sparkling wine with some world-class vintages that have won top prizes in international competitions. The chalk sub-soil in Kent and Sussex where most of the grapes for sparkling wine are grown is almost identical to that of the Champagne region. The trouble is, calling it 'English sparkling wine' is rather an inelegant mouthful – not snappy like cava or prosecco. Hampshire producer Christian Seely suggests calling it 'Britagne' (pronounced 'Britannia') but this has yet to be adopted by the industry.

Champagne gained international renown due to the proximity of Rheims cathedral where French kings were traditionally crowned and who celebrated with the eponymous sparkling wine. In the eyes of the world's nobility and *haute bourgeoisie*, champagne meant luxury and power and it became the only drink worthy of festivities, rites of passage, celebrations. It still is.

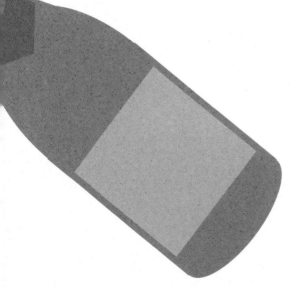

Cava is Spain's sparkling wine and derives its name from cool cellars the wine ages in. The Spanish sparkling wine tradition started in the mid-nineteenth century and was centred on Catalonia, as it still is. To be labelled cava, the wine must be made using the *méthode champenoise*; if it is not then it is *vinos espumosos*.

Prosecco is Italy's contribution to the panoply of sparkling wines. It is a light and delicate wine made from the prosecco grape (which may have originated in a village of the same name). The carbonation comes via the Charmat method, which means after primary fermentation it undergoes a secondary fermentation in bulk tanks and is bottled under pressure.

Blanquette de Limoux is considered to be the first sparkling white wine produced in France. It was first mentioned in 1531 in papers from an abbey in Saint-Hilaire – decades before the cider makers and winemakers of England reported on their experiments to create secondary fermentation in the bottle. However, the method used by the monks in Limoux was known as *méthode rurale*, which entails stopping the wine from fermenting then bottling and warming it so the first fermentation restarts. This would give the wine low alcohol and a gentle sparkle and it would have only slightly resembled wine made by the *méthode champenoise*.

Both World Wars impacted heavily on the Champagne region. Fighting during the First World War lasted more than four years and a large proportion of vines were flattened. In Rheims the network of chalk cellars normally used to store bottles of champagne were converted to subterranean barracks and field hospitals. Then during the Nazi occupation of France millions of bottles of wine and champagne were plundered. The Nazis would drink champagne to celebrate a victory, so the French Resistance kept close watch on where the loot was dispatched because this was a clue to the occupiers' military plans. British intelligence services had prior warning of the invasion of North Africa in 1941 when thousands of cases of fizz were shipped there. Producers of champagne, burgundy, and bordeaux were forced to sell their precious goods to the enemy at low prices. In order to show contempt for the occupiers, vintners relabelled poor wine as though it was a high-quality vintage. The good vino was concealed in walled-up cellars.

HOW SPARKLING WINE IS MADE

Depending on where in the world, sparkling wine producers use different grapes and methods of achieving the fizz.

In Champagne, producers can use pinot noir, pinot meunier, or chardonnay grapes. These are also used by England's leading sparkler producers and in some cases grapes such as bacchus and seyval blanc. Prosecco in Italy is made with the grape of the same name, whereas Spanish grapes such as macabeo, parellada and xarel·lo are used to make cava.

Sparkling starts off as still wine from fermented grape juice. Effervescence comes later through one of four procedures.

Méthode champenoise is the traditional process by which champagne and high-quality sparklers are produced. After primary fermentation they are bottled with yeast and sugar to trigger a secondary fermentation where carbon dioxide is produced. Then they are sealed with a 'crown cork' (beer-bottle type) metal cap, laid flat on a rack in a cellar and left to age quietly for months or years. To prepare the wine for sale the bottles are tipped upside down and gently rotated either by hand or machine in a process called *rémuage* or riddling. This causes the yeast sediment known as lees to settle in the neck of the bottle, which is then frozen. The bottle is opened and carbon dioxide pressure forces out the ice plug of lees in a process known as disgorgement (*dégorgement* in French). It is quickly topped up with *liqueur d'expédition* – wine and sugar – and sealed with the standard champagne cork.

Prosecco, Asti Spumante and other light sparklers are made using a method called *metodo Charmat* where the wine undergoes secondary fermentation in stainless steel tanks and is then bottled under pressure.

The 'transfer method' incorporates the *méthode champenoise* and when the wine has spent months in the bottle it is transferred into a tank to be filtered and if necessary blended with other wines. After this it is bottled and sold. Producers using this method are usually looking for a standardised product.

The cheapest option is 'gas injection' where the wine in tanks is injected with gas from a carbonator. Low-quality sparklers use this method. It produces large bubbles that dissipate quickly leading to unsatisfying flaccid wine.

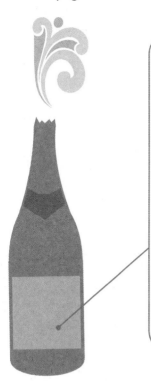

Swedish freighter *Jönköping* was torpedoed by a German U-boat in the Baltic in 1916. Amongst the cargo were 5,000 bottles of champagne (including a number of Heidsieck vintage 1907), 36,000 litres of cognac supposedly destined for the Russian army, and 6,000 litres of red wine. When it was salvaged in 1997 experts realised that conditions at the bottom of the sea were perfect for preserving champagne. Water pressure ensured the corks stayed in the bottles and a constant temperature had slowed down the aging so when the champers was tasted it was still youthful with a lively effervescence and not a hint of the sea.

A champagne bottle contains 75 cl of fizz. That's either too much or not enough for some people. Not a problem because there is a plethora of sizes to choose. Several of them are named after biblical kings. In order, from smallest to largest with the size relative to a bottle noted in brackets, they are:

Quarter a.k.a. a split (¼)

Half-bottle (½)

Bottle (1)

Magnum (2)

Jeroboam (4)

Rehoboam (6)

Methuselah (8)

Salmanazar (12)

Balthazar (16)

Nebuchadnezzar (20)

A useful mnemonic to remember how the order runs after the bottle size:
My Judy Really Makes Splendid Belching Noises.

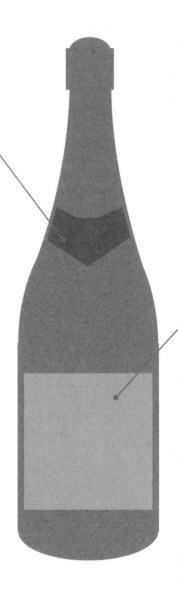

A ship launch is an occasion to celebrate and it is not complete without a bottle of champagne swung against the side of the vessel. If the bottle does not break then the craft is destined for bad luck. For millennia, ship launches were sacred rituals performed to beseech the gods to protect all who sailed in her. Before champagne became de rigueur, a precious metal goblet of wine was used. Think of the launch as a baptism ceremony – the ship's bow and deck were anointed with wine and blessings bestowed. Then the goblet was thrown overboard. By the late seventeenth century it was tradition for a bottle of wine to be smashed across the bow. Eventually that was replaced by the most elite of libations, champagne.

Champagne corks are composed of several sections. The upper portion that remains outside the bottle as the platform for the muselet is formed of ground cork and glue. This is attached to a cylinder of pristine cork that sits inside the bottle. For bottling it is compressed and inserted into the neck and over time it swells to form the distinctive mushroom shape.

ROSÉ

Pink fizz is produced either by the juice being in contact with the skins of black grapes for up to three days or with cheaper brands, by adding a small amount of still red to the sparkling wine.

SWEETNESS

Champagne and sparkling wines range from dry to sweet depending on the amount of residual sugar in the bottle and this will be specified on the label. From driest to sweetest they are: brut nature, extra brut, brut, extra dry, sec, demi-sec, doux. Today brut is the most common type.

BREAD WINE – VODKA

Most people have probably sampled liquid bread (beer); but how about bread wine? That's quite likely because bread wine was the name for vodka in Russia before the V word took off to describe a social drink rather than spirit used for medicinal tinctures. Vodka is usually made by distilling cereal hence the bread connection. The name 'vodka' may derive from the Slavic term *woda/voda*, which means 'water'. Adding the suffix 'ka' makes it a diminutive – 'little water'. This H_2O connection suggests that the description of distilled spirit as *aqua vita* or 'water of life' extended into northern Europe. In Sweden where Absolut, one of the world's leading vodka brands was born the term 'vodka' was only used from the 1950s. For centuries prior it was known as *brännvin*, which translates as 'burned wine'. Burned wine is also where the word 'brandy' originated as an English version of the Dutch word *brandewijn*.

Where was vodka first made – Russia or Poland? That depends on the nationality of the person answering the question because both nations claim to be the spiritual home of little water. Russian historians contend it originated in Russia in the fourteenth century, but the Poles say they were already making it way before then. There are written sources in Poland circa 1534 asserting that vodka could 'increase fertility and awaken lust'. No one can prove which country first distilled what was to become such a source of pride and revenue for the two countries.

Russian Tsar Ivan the Terrible established a state monopoly on vodka in the mid-sixteenth century when the only people licensed to distil it were his supporters – the *boyars* (the Russian nobility). No surprise that the production of moonshine and smuggling of poorly produced spirits became endemic with dodgy adulterated batches regularly killing people. A significant percentage of state income was raised through taxes on vodka so consumption was encouraged. When the government monopoly on vodka production was repealed in the 1860s, prices dropped and people could afford to buy even more. By the early twentieth century, almost 90 per cent of all alcohol consumed in Russia was vodka.

In post-Tsarist Russia successive generations of political leaders have celebrated or vilified vodka. Following the Bolshevik Revolution of 1917 alcohol and drunkenness were outlawed and Lenin considered it to be a social evil that prevented citizens from attaining Communist nirvana. Several Russian vodka-makers emigrated including one Mr Smirnoff who set up a small-scale distillery in Paris.

Stalin by contrast was a drinker; he revoked the ban on alcohol in 1924 and nationalised the production of vodka. As vodka was part of Russian identity, drinking it was a patriotic duty. Soviet soldiers received 100 ml per day in their standard rations (to put that in context, a British pub spirit measure is 25 ml). The intention was to keep soldiers' morale high but the result was that it whetted the appetite and industrial alcohol or anti-freeze became fair game leading to the death of many young men.

In the 1980s Mikhail Gorbachev tried to cure the epidemic of drunkenness by closing distilleries, limiting the outlets that could sell alcohol, and banning the sale of booze in restaurants before 2 p.m. To set a good example official government receptions became dry. The result of these temperance policies was similar to what had happened in the USA during Prohibition – an increase in organised crime, a surge in production of *samogon* (moonshine) and a rise in alcohol poisoning as people resorted to drinking solvents. State revenues declined to the point where extra banknotes had to be printed, which in turn spurred inflation. The campaign to cut consumption was abandoned after two years.

When Boris Yeltsin, a notoriously enthusiastic imbiber, took office in 1991 and started on a policy of economic reform, his decree 'On the Abolition of the State Monopoly on Vodka' resulted in a flood of low-quality often hazardous spirit that increased the mortality rate. Deregulation also left a hole in the coffers but when Yeltsin tried to re-establish state control the opposition from private vested interests was too strong.

Teetotaller Vladimir Putin also turned his gimlet gaze on alcohol with the intention of regulating its sale and production and restricting its consumption. This included a tax hike, prohibition on alcohol consumption in public places such as the street, and a ban on its purchase between 11 p.m. and 8 a.m. But trying to separate a Russian from his or her national drink has unintended consequences as any government around the world that has tried to regulate alcohol can attest.

Vodka flavoured with fruit, spices, or bison grass is so last century. How about bacon or smoked salmon? Both are produced in the USA and add a savoury smokiness to a cocktail. To produce this gourmet spirit, infuse a slice of bacon or salmon in ethanol alcohol and let it marinate for a few days. Filter the lumps of flesh and bingo – concentrated essence of pig or salmon! Add it to the vodka, drink and wait for the reaction…

Although the heartland of vodka is northern and eastern Europe where it is usually drunk neat, vodka is also produced in countries such as New Zealand, Japan, France and the UK. Drinkers of neat vodka will disagree with the description of it having neutral flavour but it is precisely that quality which makes it indispensable as the base for mixed drinks, such as Martini, Bloody Mary, Screwdriver, or a simple vodka and tonic. In the USA, the land of cocktails, consumption of vodka was miniscule until in the 1950s when Smirnoff's American advertising agency emphasised vodka's neutral odour and taste, but robust properties with the strapline 'It leaves you breathless'. Sales rocketed and by the mid-1970s, vodka had even overtaken sales of Uncle Sam's national drink – bourbon.

Such is vodka's universal appeal that it is the common denominator between teenagers glugging alcopops on the park bench and New Yorkers sipping cosmopolitans in swish cocktail bars.

HOW VODKA IS MADE

Vodka is made by fermenting wheat, barley, rye, rice, potatoes, sugar beet, or molasses and then distilling the alcohol into a clear, colourless liquid. This is filtered several times, usually through charcoal, to remove impurities and in the majority of vodkas pure water is added to reduce the alcohol level to around 40 per cent. Distillers make much of the provenance of the water in their products – glacier, alpine spring, artesian, deep wells – implying that the purity of the water makes their product superior. Vodka requires no aging and is ready to drink as soon as it is bottled.

Flavoured vodka is made by aromatising or infusing the spirit in fruit, herbs, spices, flowers and even grass as in the Polish speciality bison-grass vodka.

Vodka drinkers often claim not to feel grotty after a big night out because their poison is pure thanks to it being filtered. Levels of those pesky hangover causing congeners (byproducts of fermentation) are much lower. Lighter coloured beverages contain fewer congeners, whereas levels in darker coloured drinks are high. Bourbon, red wine and brandy are thought to be the worst for generating hangovers.

Horilka is a term used in the Ukraine for strong alcohol but usually refers to vodka. In his novel, *Taras Bulba*, Nikolai Gogol described it this way: 'Bring us horilka of the purest kind, give us that demon drink that makes us merry, playful and wild!'

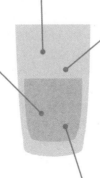

Vodka can be stored in a freezer without the bottle cracking due to the low freezing point of alcohol (between −114 °C and 0 °C depending on the water content).

Mongolian nomads traditionally drink vodka from a communal shallow silver bowl that is handed from person to person. This means the drinker can see whether the liquid is clear or cloudy because if it is the latter, it may be poisoned.

WATER OF LIFE – WHISKY

Usquebaugh pronounced 'uskwi ba' is a Gaelic translation of *aqua vitae*, the water of life, and is better known as whisky. In Scotland it is never 'whiskey' – that's how the Americans and the Irish spell it. And talking of Ireland, don't tell the Scots but the skills of how to make their national drink were probably introduced by Irish monks who arrived in the west of Scotland on a mission to convert the heathen Picts. Knowledge of distilling spread through Europe's monasteries when missionary monks travelled to spread Christianity. There is a legend that St Patrick introduced distilling into Ireland in the fifth century but no documentation to prove it.

Scotland's natives were pugnacious warrior folk who put the willies up the Romans so emphatically that they built a couple of walls (the Antonine and Hadrian's) to keep the hairy creatures contained in Caledonia. Perhaps the Picts' reputation for fearlessness was connected with their heather ale. Heather roots and stalks harbour a powdery moss called fogg that is mildly narcotic and hallucinogenic. If the Picts were tripping when they battled the Romans no wonder they won! When heather ale was distilled into what was called in Scots Gaelic *uisge beatha* using the Irish monks' new-fangled stills, there was no going back. As Scotland found its spiritual soul it also discovered the soul of its spirit.

Scotland's earliest documented evidence of distilling appeared in the Exchequer Rolls around 1494 with the entry 'Eight bolls of malt to Friar John Cor wherewith to make aqua vitae.' Friar John was based at Lindores Abbey in Fife and he had enough malt to make the modern equivalent of 1500 bottles of whisky.

The popularity of *uisge beatha* as a recreational drink rather than an elixir had the inevitable result of the exciseman coming to call. The Scottish parliament decided towards the end of the seventeenth century to tax first malted barley, and later whisky. Naturally this led to illicit distilling. Just like their counterparts in England when eighteenth-century brandy smuggling became big business, men of the cloth joined their brethren in facilitating the distribution of Scotland's national drink. Excisemen, a.k.a. the gaugers, were charged with uncovering clandestine stills and confiscated thousands each year. With the Act of Union in 1707, when Scotland and England were united, power shifted to London, and tax on whisky increased as did bloody confrontations with the excisemen. Stalemate lasted for decades as the man in the glen refused to stop making his combustible home-brew. A Scottish nobleman, the Duke of Gordon, suggested to the government that if distillers bought a licence to make it legally and then paid a set amount per gallon, the Exchequer would probably make more money from lawful whisky than they had done through years of illicit production. In 1823 the Excise Act was passed and within ten years smuggling had ceased.

In England whisky was considered to be a low rough spirit that those peasants north of the border drank to excess, or a dram to warm the cockles of gentlemen when stag hunting. It was not for consumption in respectable drawing rooms. But the sassenachs changed their opinion when in 1862 the vine louse *Phylloxera vastatrix* started to devastate vineyards including those in Cognac and supplies of brandy dwindled. Suddenly whisky was not so bad after all. It also helped that Queen Victoria was enamoured of all things Scottish and this established whisky as an essential on the drinks menu.

Nowadays Scotch contributes more than £4 billion annually to the economy with domestic consumption and worldwide exports. It has such a mythical reputation that in China it is the latest way for business people to show off their wealth and present a cultured image. Not bad for something that, little more than 140 years ago, was considered by certain people as something that only bumpkins drank.

Whisky Galore – this charming book by Compton MacKenzie from 1947, released as a film two years later – was based on a true story when a heavily laden cargo ship SS *Politician* bound for the USA ran aground near the Outer Hebrides island of Eriskay during a storm. When the locals discovered that 260,000 bottles of duty-free Scotch were stored in the ship's hold they thought it was heaven on earth because whisky was scarce due to wartime rationing. Under cover of darkness, islanders rowed out to the wreck and boarded the ship then took up to 24,000 bottles before Customs & Excise officials arrived to spoil the party and blow up the ship's hull to stop the scavenging. Islanders had to drink the evidence or secrete the stash by burying it or hiding it down rabbit holes so they were not prosecuted when the police came knocking. The bounty lasted for years and even now booty is occasionally discovered and the odd bottle washes up on a beach. The book's title is a pun on the Scottish Gaelic phrase *gu leòir* meaning 'plenty'.

The 'angels' share' is the spirit that evaporates from oak casks during years of maturation. Hot, dry conditions increase evaporation, so storage warehouses are normally cool and damp. Oak is semi-porous and the whisky interacts with outside elements leading to oxidation. This reduces harshness, adds character and increases complexity. But this porosity also means a proportion of the 'water of life' disappears. HM Revenue & Customs permits evaporation of 2 per cent volume per annum untaxed. During a ten-year maturation that equates to 50 litres surrendered to the heavens.

A batch of raw spirit for whisky can be made in less than a week but to be legally called Scotch it must mature in Scotland in oak casks for at least three years. Most single malt whiskies are aged for around a decade. Once it is bottled, whisky does not mature so a ten year old will always be a ten year old.

HOW SCOTCH WHISKY IS MADE

Place peat-smoked malted cereal (usually barley) into a mash tun and mash it with hot water so the malt starch converts to sugars. The run-off is called wort and this is transferred to a fermenting vessel where yeast is added. The yeast ferments the sugars producing alcohol and carbon dioxide.

The fermented liquid is transferred into a copper still and boiled so the alcohol evaporates into the neck of the still where it condenses. Typically it is distilled twice. At this point the clear spirit is *eau de vie* and cannot legally be called Scotch whisky until it has matured for at least three years in an oak cask. The cask may previously have contained sherry, wine, Madeira, port, or American bourbon. During the maturation period in cool cellars or warehouses the oak imparts colour, aroma and flavour to the spirit. The immediate environment can also have an influence as the casks breathe and draw in air so, for instance, if a distillery is on a coast the whisky may have a salt or iodine tang. When the *eau de vie* has aged for the prescribed time it is bottled. Single malt is the product of one specific distillery whereas blended Scotch may be a combination of whiskies from several different distilleries.

Scotland's bard, Robert Burns, he who inspires the annual evening of whisky sozzling on 25 January (Burn's Night), worked from 1789 until his death in 1796 as one of the despised excisemen with responsibility to collect taxes and catch smugglers. It is safe to say that this was a job of convenience rather than conviction because of the 1792 subject of one of his poems, *'The Deil's Awa wi' th' Exciseman'* (The Devil has Taken the Exciseman).

Scientists at the New Zealand Antarctic Trust were surprised to unearth five crates of whisky and brandy buried for over 100 years underneath the hut of the explorer Ernest Shackleton. As some of the crates had cracked and ice formed inside, it was a delicate task to extract the contents for a very important experiment – to recreate the original Mackinlay whisky recipe. It took almost four years from discovering the bottles to transporting and slowly thawing them, conducting scientific analysis, then distilling and ageing the recreated whisky at the Whyte & MacKay distillery. Anyone who wants a taste of what Shackleton and his men would have experienced during their expedition will find a delicate and light whisky with aromas of apple, pear, pineapple, marmalade, and spice. Bottles are on sale with a percentage of profits going to the Antarctic Heritage Trust.

Peatreek: the Lowland Scots word for 'smoke' is 'reek'. Illicit moonshine was nicknamed 'peatreek' – a reference to the peat used to malt the grain.

'Awakening the serpent' is what whisky drinkers call the phenomenon of viscimation where liquids of different viscosities mix and create visible eddies and ribbons.

Money has always been required to fund the campaigns of Americans running for political office. Even from the beginning of the republic, candidates needed deep pockets because people who came out to vote expected to be rewarded with whiskey and plenty of it. Unless they went home tipsy, the politician was not considered to be civic minded and therefore was unsuitable for public office.

Mark Twain said: *'Too much of anything is bad but too much of good whiskey is barely enough.'*

BLENDED WHISKY

Some people are snooty about blended whisky, revering single malts instead. But without the success of major brands such as Famous Grouse that buy the whiskies they blend from a number of distilleries, some of those smaller operations might not survive and their celebrated single malts would no longer be produced. To virgin palates blended whisky is often smoother, lighter and easier to drink than single malts.

Blended Scotch is a mix of dozens of different single malts combined with grain whisky (which is made with cereals other than barley and distilled using a different method). Each of these whiskies has a unique character that contributes to the personality of the blend.

Until demand for Scotch – especially in England – increased in the nineteenth century and hastened the use of glass bottles, whisky was sold in casks or stoneware jars known as pigs and decanted at home. As business flourished in the blending houses they started to label their product and sell it in bottles so names such as Bell's, Teacher's and Johnnie Walker earned a worldwide reputation for quality. Even today, as one whisky writer put it, single malt gets all of the glory but the blends pay the bills.

WHISKEY IN AMERICA

Early immigrants to America were Scottish, Scots Irish (from Ulster) and Irish who took with them to the New World an independent outlook, distrust of government, their national drink, whisk(e)y and the skills to distil it. Settling particularly in Pennsylvania, Maryland, and West Virginia the pioneers were small-scale farmers scratching a living growing corn and rye. Both cereals could be distilled into whiskey and by the time of the American Declaration of Independence in 1776 there were countless stills in the nascent republic. The revolutionary war with Britain depleted America's cash reserves and when in the early 1790s the federal government levied a tax on spirits to help pay off the national debt, there was trouble at t' mill. Whiskey was not just a drink, and part of the settlers' heritage, it was also used as currency to barter with and was intrinsic to their culture. In what became known as the Whiskey Rebellion, excisemen who tried to collect the taxes, or the people who paid them, were attacked by violent mobs in western Pennsylvania and beaten, sometimes tarred and feathered, and even killed. The Whiskey Boys, as they became known, even talked of declaring independence. They had not cast off the shackles of one tax-crazy power only to live under the tyranny of another one in Washington DC. In 1794 the federal government sent an army of around 13,000 soldiers to quell the insurrection. It was led by President George Washington, who issued a proclamation which included this paragraph:

> *And whereas, it is in my judgment necessary under the circumstances of the case to take measures for calling forth the militia in order to suppress the combinations aforesaid, and to cause the laws to be duly executed; and I have accordingly determined so to do, feeling the deepest regret for the occasion, but withal the most solemn conviction that the essential interests of the Union demand it, that the very existence of government and the fundamental principles of social order are materially involved in the issue, and that the patriotism and firmness of all good citizens are seriously called upon, as occasions may require, to aid in the effectual suppression of so fatal a spirit.*

Order was peacefully restored when the rebels stood down and went home after the ringleaders were arrested (later pardoned). This experience of government interference prompted migration further into the interior and many settled in Kentucky and Tennessee where they found smooth, limestone-filtered water and country ideal for growing corn. Behold the birth of bourbon!

An Act of Congress in 1964 proclaimed bourbon as the official spirit of the United States of America. To be called bourbon it must be made in the USA (any state), contain at least 51 per cent corn and be stored for at least two years in new, charred oak barrels. Bourbon county in Kentucky was originally French territory and was named after the Kings of France.

American whiskey is commonly divided into six categories: bourbon, Tennessee, rye, wheat, corn and blended whiskey – the differences being largely in the type or amount of cereal used in production.

Tennessee whiskey is similar in taste to bourbon but must be produced in the state of Tennessee and filtered through sugar-maple charcoal. Jack Daniel's is the best known although ironically, in a hangover from the years of Prohibition, the distillery is situated in Moore county which is 'dry' – meaning that the most famous product in the state can only be consumed at home and not in public.

When the American coopers' union persuaded the distilling industry to use a new cask for each barrel of bourbon or whiskey they could not have known what a boon that was for distillers of Scotch. The previously used American casks are taken apart, shipped to Scotland as bundles called shooks and the staves reassembled. American oak in which bourbon or rye whiskey has aged imparts highly desirable flavours to the Scotch.

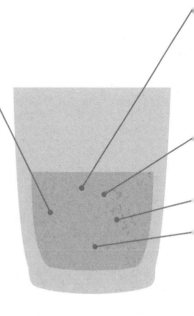

A manhattan is a classic cocktail made from whiskey, sweet vermouth and bitters so it is appropriate that the name of the eponymous New York island may derive from alcohol. According to the *Encyclopaedia of New York City*, Manhattan might stem from a Native American word. When explorer Henry Hudson visited the island in 1609 he met some of the Lenape natives and invited them to have a drink. They were unused to alcohol and quickly became intoxicated. When Hudson asked them the name of the island one of them is reputed to have replied *manahachtanienk*. The word translates as 'place of general inebriation'. There are two more prosaic explanations of the origin of the name and both of them derive from Lenape Unami words: (a) *menatay* (island), and (b) *manahatouh* (place where timber is procured for bows and arrows). Take your pick.

In many Latin American countries instead of saying 'cheese' to form a smile when being photographed, people say 'whisky'.

In the phonetic alphabet Whiskey is used to represent the letter 'W'.

Winston Churchill saw action as a soldier in the Sudan and the Boer War and said: 'The water was not fit to drink. To make it palatable we had to add whisky. By diligent effort I learnt to like it.'

HOW TO TASTE WHISKY

Beer, cider, and wine can be tasted in a similar way but whisky has its own method.

Use a copita or snifter with a narrow opening so the aromas are concentrated – a brandy balloon works too. Tilt the glass to forty-five degrees and rotate it gently one full turn then hold it vertically. A ring will appear where the whisky has touched the side of the glass and over a few seconds little beads appear. These are called legs or tears.

Sniff the whisky several times then pause to breathe in fresh air. At first the alcohol will smell strongly and make the eyes water. Gently turn the whisky once round the glass. After a few sniffs the nose becomes accustomed and can start to identify the aromas. Keep going back for more.

Sip the whisky so it coats the mouth – this acclimatises the palate to the spirit. Take another drop and hold it on the tongue. The aromas will enter the olfactory glands through the mouth and hit the brain a few seconds later. Chew the whisky for four or five seconds; this will release more flavours. Sensory scientists have identified over 400 flavour compounds in whisky and depending on the brand and the casks it is matured in it may have heather, honey, vanilla, leather, tobacco, marmalade, smoke, iodine, or fruit characteristics.

Notice the texture and mouth-feel of the whisky. Is it smooth, viscous, mouth-coating? Fresh, acerbic, mouth-drying? Creamy? Full-bodied, thin? Swallow the whisky slowly and think about the flavours in the 'finish' (the aftertaste).

Now try an experiment with the same whisky. Add two drops of still water – don't drown it! This will open it up and change its character by releasing different aromas and flavours. It may even taste like a different whisky.

SCOTCH WHISKY REGIONS

The Scotch Whisky Association recognises five distinct whisky-distilling regions.

The Highlands: the area of Scotland north of a line from Dundee on the North Sea coast to Greenock on the west, including all of the islands except for Islay. Because it is such a large region the character of the whisky varies. In the far north they tend to be light bodied with a spicy character; central, southern and eastern whiskies are generally light bodied, fruity and sweet. Celebrated brands include Dalmore and Glenmorangie.

Speyside: a tiny area on the Moray coast which has more distilleries than anywhere else in Scotland including the world's two best-selling single malt brands Glenlivet and Glenfiddich. Whiskies from this region vary but can generally be divided into two categories: either heavy and rich, or complex, light and floral.

The Lowlands: encompass the Scottish mainland south of the Highlands except the Mull of Kintyre. Amongst the whiskies of this region are Auchentoshan and Glenkinchie. Whisky from this region is good for beginners and tends to be mellow and easy to drink.

Islay: an island off the west coast. Whiskies from Islay are unmistakable – intensely smoky with a distinctive medicinal tang that is said to come from sea salt permeating the local peat that is used to malt the barley. Ardbeg and Laphroaig are two of the best known.

Campbeltown: a port on the tip of the Mull of Kintyre on the southwest coast of Scotland with three distilleries; Springbank, Glen Gyle, and Glen Scotia. Whiskies from there have a distinctive spicy and salty tinge.

A NECESSITY OF LIFE – WINE

Unlike most other alcoholic drinks, which need human intervention, wine could make itself. That little grape is self-sufficient with a sac of sugar on the inside, and outside on the skin a colony of yeasts just waiting to drill through the membrane and consume the delicious juice to deliver alcohol through fermentation. How could something as humble as a few bunches of berries earn so much respect? In ancient societies such as Greece and Rome, wine engendered a sense of exceptionalism. Wine drinkers were civilised, unlike the barbarians abroad who drank the fermented juice of barley rather than grape. Wine was a high-status libation, a gift from the gods that inspired poetry and rhapsody and quotes such as 'If God forbade drinking, would He have made wine so good?' (Cardinal Richelieu). The extraordinary thing after several millennia is that wine still has the reputation of being the refined choice and beer the drink of the common man.

So where was the wine first made? As we saw in the earlier section on Mesopotamia, the earliest evidence so far discovered points to residents of a village called Hajji Firuz Tepe in the Zagros Mountains (modern Iran) who were enjoying a snifter between 5400 and 5000 BC. Pottery jars unearthed by archaeologists show traces of wine made from grapes. This Neolithic wine had also contained resin from the terebinth tree, added possibly as a preservative or for medicinal purposes. Wild grapes still flourish today in the Zagros mountains and some archaeologists believe that the first domesticated grapevines grew in this area. By 3000 BC cultivated vines had been transplanted to the Jordan valley, and other societies in the Middle East such as Ancient Egypt were introduced to the joy of fermented grape juice.

Armenia is north of the Zagros mountains and in 2010 a team of archaeologists discovered the world's oldest-known winery in a cave near the village of Areni. This kit, dating to about 4100 BC, included proof of everything required to make wine – withered vines, skins and seeds, a press for trampling grapes under foot, a trough for the juice to run into vats to ferment, storage vessels and most importantly – drinking cups. The cave's dry and cool conditions would have made the perfect wine cellar.

Today winemakers still use similar principles as those Stone Age vintners. It all starts with the harvest of perfectly ripened grapes – under-ripe or over-ripe and the wine will not be good. Picking by hand is increasingly being replaced by machine harvesting. Back in the winery, humans sort the grapes for quality and remove any substandard fruit. Traditional wineries will crush the grapes by foot but most commercial ones use automated presses. The grapes are treated differently depending on whether red, white or rosé wine is being made. With few exceptions, when making white wine the skins are separated from the grape pulp and only the juice (known as 'must') goes into a fermenting tank; whereas with red and rosé the grapes are macerated, meaning that the juice is in contact with the skins and pips as these impart colour, tannins, texture, and flavour compounds. For rosé this will be one to three days, and red wine can be up to four weeks. With red wine the longer the must is in contact with the skins and pips the 'bigger' the wine is likely to be.

When it is time for the miracle of juice to turn into wine as yeast ferments the sugars the vintner has a choice. Some will rely on the yeast in the grape skins or atmosphere around the winery to do the trick but the big brands want a more predictable outcome so they add cultured yeasts. To reduce the wine's acidity, lactic acid bacteria may be added and this converts malic acid (harsh and mouth puckering) into lactic acid to produce a softer mouth feel. This process is known as malolactic fermentation.

Wine is matured in oak barrels or stainless steel tanks to develop complexity. The latter is not as romantic as the former and is rather clinical but it creates a standardised wine that vintners with major commercial brands seek. To compensate for the desirable effect that oak aging gives to wine, producers can cheat and throw oak chips into the tank. Before bottling, egg white, or isinglass (collagen from the air bladder inside a tropical fish) finings are added to bind with any unwanted solids such as yeast cells and make them easy to remove. The wine is filtered so it is no longer cloudy and will be attractive on the eye in the bottle and glass. After bottling (depending on the wine) it is ready to drink immediately or it is stored in a cool dark cellar to age and improve.

Wine was the first international drink and its reputation spread with missionary zeal from those first vintners in the Caucasus to the Middle East and Mediterranean rim. From there Phoenician, ancient Greek and Roman oenophiles took it far and wide, and where possible vines were planted to establish viticulture in countries they colonised or traded with. Spanish conquistadors transported vines to the Americas, Dutch traders established viticulture in South Africa, and British colonists planted vineyards in Australasia. Today wine is even produced in India, China and Japan from locally grown grapes. In case of emergency this is how to ask for a bottle of wine in Tokyo: 'Kon nichi wa. Wain hitobin dozo. Arigato'.

During the First World War, Allied soldiers posted in France mangled the pronunciation of *vin blanc* and came up with 'plink plonk' or 'plonk' for short. Nowadays plonk refers to cheap wine that is very near the grape.

Some wines such as Sauternes and Tokay owe their sweet character to a fungus called *Botrytis cinerea* which in the right circumstances (dry weather) can cause grapes on the vine to shrivel thereby concentrating the sugars and investing an intense honey aroma and flavour in the wine. Noble rot is another name for this occurrence and may sound pejorative but to viticulturalists who produce highly sought-after dessert wines it is a gift of nature.

That concave dimple at the bottom of most wine bottles is known as a punt. The most likely origin of the word is from the Italian *puntello* – the iron rod on which a hand-blown glass bottle was fashioned. When the bottle was removed from the *puntello* it would leave a rough scar. An indentation was made so the bottle could stand up without falling over. It is now a historical remnant with no practical use.

The rapture of wine has inspired quotes such as:

- *'In Vino Veritas'* which translates as 'In wine there is truth': Pliny the Elder (AD 23–75), first-century Roman naturalist and philosopher.

- *'Wine is fit for man in a wonderful way provided that it is taken with good sense by the sick as well as the healthy'*: Hippocrates (c.460–370 BC) Ancient Greek physician.

- *'Wine is the healthiest, most hygienic beverage known to man'*: Louis Pasteur, French chemist.

- *'A man will be eloquent if you give him good wine'*: American writer Ralph Waldo Emerson.

- *'Good wine is a necessity of life for me'*: Thomas Jefferson, American Founding Father.

- *'I was able to drink a good deal of wine and to bear it well'*: engraved on the tomb of fifth-century BC Persian king, Darius I.

Would you Adam and Eve it – £105,000 for a bottle of wine? In 1985 that was the price of the most expensive bottle ever sold. But this was not just any wine, it was a bottle of 1787 Château Lafite engraved with the initials of Thomas Jefferson, Founding Father of the United States of America. When noted oenophile Jefferson was Ambassador to France (1784–1789) he spent much time visiting vineyards to buy wine for his own collection and for friends at home. The record-breaking wine would be undrinkable but that was not the intention – it was purchased for the Forbes Collection in New York as a piece of Jefferson memorabilia.

Another alleged Thomas Jefferson wine collection turned out to be rather overpriced when American industrialist and collector William Koch paid around $310,000 in 1988 for four bottles of red wine etched with the initials 'Th J' said to date from 1787. When Koch became suspicious of the wine's provenance, experts examined the bottles and concluded the etching had been done with a twentieth-century electric power tool.

Terroir is a French term from *terre* (land) which refers to the unique influence that local soil, climate, and geology has on plants such as grapes. Compare a New World wine with an Old World one made from the same varietal and the effect of *terroir* is apparent.

Wine used for religious sacraments such as Holy Communion is usually red, sweet and alcoholic unless – as in faiths such as Methodists and Evangelical Christians – alcohol is frowned upon. In those cases, they use grape juice. Some wineries were founded specifically to produce wine for use in church or temple. The oldest vineyard still producing altar wine is O-Neh-Da in New York State, founded in 1872.

White wine can be made with white or black grapes because the juice only is used to make white wine. Red and rosé can only be made with black grapes as it is the skin that gives the wine its colour.

Blending grapes permits winemakers to make better wine than some single varietals on their own would make. Popular blends include Sauvignon Blanc with Sémillon, where the former supplies acidity to complement the latter's mellow rounded fullness.

Glassware can enhance wine. An ideal wine glass has a large bowl with tapered sides. This concentrates aroma as the wine is swirled, allows it to breathe and often softens wines with sharp tannins. A narrow rim at the top of the glass improves acidic wines and generally enhances aromas. A long stem prevents the hand from warming the wine.

Professional tasters spit out wine not because this is a special technique but because they may be tasting dozens of wine in a session and do not want to become tipsy.

More than 98 per cent of British people have never tasted a wine made from grapes grown in Blighty yet there are over 400 vineyards in England and Wales. Scotland does not yet have a commercial grape wine industry although some tasty fruit wines are produced there. Geographically Britain is above the latitude where grapes grow – normally between thirty and fifty degrees north and south of the equator. However, the Gulf Stream makes the climate temperate enough for viticulture although it is a challenge to ripen the grapes and for them to have a high enough sugar content if the sun does not shine sufficiently.

The climate may have been warmer in the first millennia AD. Romans planted vines during their 350-year occupation of Britain although they may have been ornamental only as wine was imported from other parts of the empire. After Christianity was introduced in the sixth century AD monasteries made wine for sacramental rituals from grapes grown in their own vineyards. Production was boosted after the Norman invasion of 1066. Forty-six vineyards were listed in the Domesday survey (late eleventh century). When the Little Ice Age set in at the end of the fourteenth century, vineyards disappeared and viticulture in Britain was not commercially viable until the twentieth century when the current revival started.

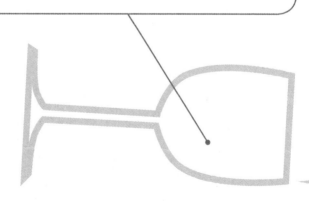

Devastation arrived in France in 1862 when a wine producer planted American vines in his Rhône vineyard and unwittingly introduced a ravenous aphid called *Phylloxera vastatrix* that breeds with astonishing speed. A single female can produce up to 26 billion offspring in eight months. *Phylloxera vastatrix* lived up to its nickname 'the dry-leaf devastator' and within months had spread throughout Europe feeding on the roots of its host. Millions of hectares of vines were destroyed creating an agrarian disaster.

The French Ministry of Agriculture offered a huge reward to anyone who could cure the blight. Hundreds of folk remedies were proposed including holy water, human urine, a cocktail of petrol and whale oil, bones dissolved in sulphuric acid, volcanic ash from Pompeii, powdered tobacco, and live toads planted in the roots to draw out the poison. Only one thing worked. The solution was the source of the problem itself, so US rootstock was grafted on to the ailing European vines because American vines had become immune to *Phylloxera*. It took years for the European wine industry to recover although this was in part due to chauvinistic old-world vintners (particularly in France) who could not bear the idea of tainting their precious vines with American ones. Large scale replanting of French vineyards did not begin until the 1890s, thirty years after *Phylloxera* had first arrived.

In wine terms 'vintage' signifies the wine was made with grapes from a single year's growth. Non-vintage means the wine is a blend of grapes from different years.

Australia is the world's fourth-largest wine exporter. From little acorns grow mighty oaks and those acorns were vines from South Africa's Cape that arrived with the First Fleet when the colony was founded in 1788. It was several decades before the wine was high enough quality for export but then production boomed – especially when the New South Wales government decreed that retailers did not require a licence to sell wine. This action was intended to wean the population off rum and reduce the trouble it caused. It did not work and Aussies carried on with their rumbustious behaviour.

When an Australian wine tasted blind at the Vienna Exhibition 1873 was highly praised, the French judges withdrew once the provenance was revealed. They protested that a wine of such quality must be from France and nowhere else, and that someone was cheating.

A modern-day butler is the most senior of the domestic staff that run large houses. Originally this role was confined to caring for and serving the wine and in English they were known as 'bottlers' from Old French *bouteillier*.

King Henry VIII was, according to a French spy in his court, regularly intoxicated. No surprise considering the drinks bill for his main residence Hampton Court Palace. Two brewers (one for unhopped ale and one for hopped beer) worked on site to supply the royal household. The lowliest courtier received four pints a day, whilst dukes had a two-gallon daily allocation making a total consumption of 600,000 gallons a year. Wine was also high on the agenda with thousands of gallons consumed annually. The wine cellars had two locks on the doors and for extra security the keys were held by two different officials of the house.

In 2010 Hampton Court Palace built a recreation of a sixteenth-century fountain that had dispensed wine. It was based on one featured in a painting of the meeting between Henry and the French King Francis I in 1520 known as the *Field of the Cloth of Gold*. Instead of water, when people dipped their cup they filled it with wine. Constructed of timber, lead, bronze and gold leaf it stood four metres high and was decorated with forty golden lions' heads, eight brass taps and a motto written in gilded letters: *'faicte bonne chere quy vouldra'* meaning 'let he who wyshes make good cheere'.

The USA's national anthem, 'The Star Spangled Banner', is not an original tune. It was originally a popular British drinking ditty called 'The Anacreontic Song'. Each verse in the original composition ends with the line 'the myrtle of Venus with Bacchus's vine'. The Anacreontic Society was a gentlemen's club in eighteenth century London named after the ancient Greek poet Anacreon celebrated for his poems on love and wine.

Snake wine has no acquaintance with grapes. It is an elixir in Chinese traditional medicine believed to have restorative properties. To make it, venomous snakes are gutted and steeped in alcohol spirit for several years. Those of an impatient nature can drink it fresh. This entails squeezing the bile from the gall bladder of a living snake into a glass and adding alcohol. Just as people choose their wine by grape variety so drinkers of this potion take their pick of snake depending on the ailment – viper or cobra.

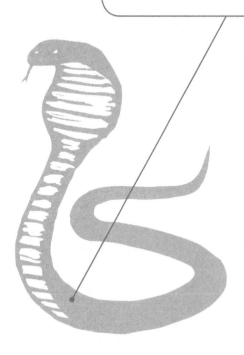

CHAPTER SIX:

THE OTHER SIDE OF THE COIN

SPEAK EASY – TEMPERANCE AND PROHIBITION

Various governments throughout history have experimented with the prohibition of alcohol, usually with little effect. The best known example of alcohol being banned where it was formerly legal is the USA, which tried the 'Noble Experiment' between 1919 and 1933.

Since the mid-nineteenth century American legislators had been under pressure from active temperance societies such as the Women's Christian Temperance Union and the Anti-Saloon League. Both organisations blamed alcohol for crime, immoral behaviour and the breakdown of society. In 1841 the Washington Temperance Society published a parody of the Declaration of Independence: 'We hold these truths to be self-evident. That all men are created temperate; that they are endowed by their creator with certain natural and innocent desires; that among these are appetites for cold water and the pursuit of happiness.'

They were not joking. But for some campaigners abstinence was not enough – an outright ban was the only course of action. They were so persuasive that the US Senate eventually ratified the Eighteenth Amendment to the Constitution in 1919, and in January 1920 the National Prohibition Act came into force.

Production of moonshine and bootlegging became rampant and there were insufficient police officers to enforce the law. Speakeasies proliferated, supplied with illegal hooch by gangsters such as Al Capone, and rumour had it also by employees of Joseph Kennedy, father of the future US President. Prohibition failed to prevent people consuming alcohol leading instead to the unintended consequences of political corruption, smuggling, deaths from adulterated booze, and a rise in organised crime.

Temperance movements proclaimed that drinking was a sin so it was rather inconvenient that wine is mentioned over 200 times in the Old Testament of the Bible and described as a gift from God. The solution was to rewrite the holy book and either remove all references to alcohol or change its use. In the King James Version of the Bible, 1 Timothy 5:23 reads 'Drink no longer water, but use a little wine for thy stomach's sake, and thine often infirmities'. The temperance version advised readers with stomach ailments to rub alcohol on their abdomens. When it came to Jesus drinking wine this was altered to unfermented grape juice instead.

In the UK abstainers in the nineteenth-century temperance movement had to pay higher life assurance premiums because in an era when outbreaks of cholera were common and water was often polluted, by not drinking alcohol they were considered to be taking risks with their health.

Teetotallers abstain completely from drinking alcohol. The term is not connected with the consumption of tea but is thought to originate in the nineteenth-century temperance movement when members signed a pledge card proclaiming 'Total Abstinence'.

By the time of the Great Depression it was apparent that consumption of alcohol had not decreased during Prohibition; it was costing too much to police, and the government was missing out on millions of dollars of liquor taxes. The law was repealed in 1933. However, even today there are still dozens of dry counties across the USA where the sale and purchase of alcohol is restricted.

William McCoy was a purveyor of high-quality bootlegged booze during US Prohibition (1920–1933). He conducted business from boats moored three miles off the coast beyond the jurisdiction of US law. Small craft would sail up to the floating off-licences and throw rolls of dollars on board in exchange for the booty. The three-mile boundary of US territorial waters became known as the Rum Line and the waiting boats branded Rum Row. Some sources claim that McCoy was the inspiration for the idiom 'the Real McCoy' in that he sold the best hooch. However a Scotch whisky company called MacKay had promoted their brand as 'the real MacKay' since 1870. Maybe 'the Real McCoy' was a pun on an already well-known phrase.

Bootlegging is a euphemism for selling or transporting illegal alcohol. Two similar theories to explain its etymology include soldiers in the American Civil War who brought bottles of whiskey into army camps by concealing them down their trousers; or the habit of people hiding illicit flasks of hooch in their boots during Prohibition.

Booze cruises proliferated during Prohibition when people would sign up for 'cruises to nowhere'. The ships headed for international waters where people could legally consume alcohol as the craft sailed aimlessly in circles.

Although the term 'cocktail' was first recorded in America in 1806, cocktails became indispensable during Prohibition when bathtub gin was made more palatable by mixing in other ingredients. Americans threw cocktail parties at home or visited speakeasies to drink secretly beyond the eyes of the law. To gain admittance to a speakeasy one had to whisper a code word through a slot in the door. American distillers of moonshine tried to improve the flavour of their spirit by adding dead rats. They were following the habit of seventeenth- and eighteenth-century British brewers who added dead cock birds stuffed with fruit and spices to the brew to add flavour. It was called cock ale. Is this where the word 'cocktail' came from?

Some people were so determined to have a drink that they were willing to take a risk by consuming industrial alcohol. To prevent the temptation of folk drinking solvent cocktails, the authorities instructed producers to add foul-tasting chemicals. It did not work as bootleggers learned how to neutralise the contaminants and customers forced themselves to live with the bad taste.

CHAPTER SEVEN:

BOTTOMS UP!

Imagine life if humans had never discovered alcohol. For a start we might no longer exist – wiped out instead by pathogens in water and with no weapons to fight them. The American Revolution may not have happened when it did; ships would be launched with bottles of water smashed against the bow; the phonetic alphabet would need another word to represent 'W'; there would be huge deficits in tax receipts of governments around the world, but more than anything, we would be going to the caff for a drinkie instead of the pub. This book would have been called 'School of Tea' and, devotee as I am of that particular brew, it cannot match the fun, companionship, and karaoke performances I have experienced when having an alcoholic libation with friends.

This book is dedicated to the British boozer – the favourite institution of countless people. How lucky are residents of these isles to have at the centre of our society public establishments that offer pleasure, refuge, sustenance, entertainment, shelter, and a free visit to the loo? Tourists from overseas report that a trip to a pub is in the top five activities they want to do during their visit to Blighty. Perhaps they will see you there. If so, maybe you would suggest they buy this book to learn about the extraordinary influence alcohol has had on human development and history and the imagination and inspiration it has borne?

In the words of Ancient Roman poet Horace: 'No poems can live long or please that are written by water-drinkers'.

Now you have read this book you are equipped with enough knowledge to regale your mates at the bar and answer correctly every booze question in the pub quiz. Can I join your team please?

Here is a challenge. If you see me in the pub and can answer this question correctly I'll buy you a drink. What was I sipping when I wrote this sentence? But beware – get it wrong and you have to buy me a pint. Bottoms up!